Winning Texas Hold'em

Library of Congress Cataloging-in-Publication Data Available

2 4 6 8 10 9 7 5 3

Published by Sterling Publishing Co., Inc.
387 Park Avenue South, New York, NY 10016

Distributed in Canada by Sterling Publishing
c/o Canadian Manda Group, 165 Dufferin Street
Toronto, Ontario, Canada M6K 3H6
Distributed in the United Kingdom by GMC Distribution
Services, Castle Place, 166 High Street, Lewes, East
Sussex, England BN7 1XU
Distributed in Australia by Capricorn Link (Australia) Pty. Ltd.
P.O. Box 704, Windsor, NSW 2756, Australia

Printed in China

Sterling ISBN-10: 1-4027-2963-4
ISBN-13: 978-1-4027-2963-8

For information about custom editions, special sales, premium and
corporate purchases, please contact Sterling Special Sales
Department at 800-805-5489 or specialsales@sterlingpub.com.

Winning Texas Hold'em

Cash Game Poker Strategies for Players of All Skill Levels

by Matt Maroon

Sterling Publishing Co., Inc.
New York

Dedication

To Vicki, for sticking by her degenerate gambler through the good swings and the bad and for always being the ace up my sleeve.

Acknowledgments

I would like to thank my family for passing on those gambling genes and for being more supportive than I ever dreamed possible. I also thank my friends for learning the game along with me—without our little brain trust, I wouldn't be half the player I am today. My thanks to David D. for putting this together in the first place and to Greg D. at Venture Literary for keeping me on task despite the doubts, and for helping me navigate the rather confusing world of publishing. Finally, my thanks to God for giving me the many opportunities that have presented themselves to me over the last few years.

CONTENTS

FOREWORD

Whatever you do, do it with all your might.
Work at it, early and late, in season and out of season,
not leaving a stone unturned, and never deferring for a single
hour that which can be done just as well now.

—P. T. Barnum

Three years ago, poker was considered a dying game. Casinos everywhere were removing poker tables and replacing them with slot machines. Card room attendance was flat, and in some places declining. Competitors at the game's flagship tournament, the World Series of Poker championship event, increased by less than 5 percent the year before. Only one or two poker tournaments wound up on TV, and they were shown just a few times annually, generally in the wee hours of the morning.

And then lightning struck. The World Poker Tour debuted on the Travel Channel and quickly became the channel's highest-rated program. It was the first regular poker show in America to feature a tiny camera exposing the players' hidden hole cards, turning the game into an exciting spectator sport. Entries to the 2003 World Series of Poker increased by over 30 percent; the event was played relentlessly on ESPN and was won by an amateur who had never played in a live poker tournament. The first prize was $2.5 million.

Over the next year poker, fueled by televised tournaments, began to grow. Card rooms were packed with waiting

lists a mile long. Sales of poker books rocketed, and Internet poker sites offering advice, some of it decent but most of it bad, sprouted like weeds. Internet card rooms advertised on televised poker events, and the number of players playing online increased every month.

In 2004, the World Series main event more than tripled its entries, from 839 to 2,576, and awarded a $5 million first prize. Casinos that had removed poker rooms in favor of slot machines and table games put them back up as quickly as they had taken them down. And players who had learned the game before the great boom (myself included) suddenly found a money tree in their backyard.

Perhaps the most important effect television has had on poker is to establish it as a game of skill. There was a time when most people thought it merely a gambling game despite the many mathematicians who had written books to the contrary. A few states such as California had actually legalized poker as a game of skill but most of the nation still considered it gambling.

I suppose for most people poker is merely gambling. Many people play poker purely for the enjoyment and don't mind that they will lose a little doing so. Often they will lose much less than they would at a slot machine or a roulette wheel and get more enjoyment out of it in the process. If you are one of those players, that's fine. But if you were one of those players, chances are you wouldn't have picked up this book.

You picked up this book because you know that poker is a game of skill. Texas Hold'em, which is by far the most popular poker game being played today, is an excellent opportunity. It provides both a rewarding hobby and, for its best players, a solid second (or perhaps even primary) income. Through the game of poker you can also learn valuable life skills, and entire books have been written about applying poker logic to many of life's problems. And you will meet a lot of interesting people.

Whether you are already a competent player seeking a little improvement for your game or a rank newbie who wants to start out the right way, this book is for you. The advice here is solid and time tested. I have used it to win a fortune at poker, and many others have as well. It comes from my many years of playing and studying the great game of hold'em. I hope it helps you as much as it has helped me. Thank you for reading and good luck!

About the Author

Matt Maroon has derived a significant portion of his income from poker for the last seven years. He learned the game as a college student at the University of Akron. After careful study of the game and plenty of hours at the tables, he quickly found his poker winnings eclipsing the amount he made at his job and decided to give the poker life a shot.

He began his poker career by playing \$3/\$6 hold'em at charity games around his home town of Akron, Ohio. After a few years he outgrew the Las Vegas Nights and now spends much of his time playing higher stakes games online and traveling around the world playing in high stakes cash games and tournaments. Limit hold'em is his best game and the topic he chose for this, his first book.

Matt still resides in Akron, where he lives with his girlfriend and more pets than he can count. He can be found anywhere there is a good game or at his personal website: www.mattmaroon.com. There you can find an assortment of helpful hints and how to's and his very popular poker blog, where he chronicles his day-to-day poker playing. Feel free to visit the site or drop him an email.

A NOTE ON READING THIS BOOK

Is this gambling?
Not the way I play it.
—W.C. FIELDS

This book is intended for readers of all skill levels. Even very advanced players can learn a considerable amount from this material, particularly in the section on short-handed play. I am writing it, however, so that it is accessible to even the newest player.

If you see a word you don't understand, I have included a glossary for your reference. Poker has a language all its own, and I will try my best to clarify it for you. After reading this book, even the newest player will be complaining about "bad beats" on "the river" like an old pro.

Here is a list of fairly common hand-naming practices that I'll be using frequently:

Ace will be denoted as A. King will be K, Queen will be Q, Jack will be J, and Ten will bc T. All others will simply use their number. So pocket aces will be denoted as AA, king ten will be denoted as KT, etc.

If a hand is suited (both cards are of the same suit) it will be denoted by an "s" following the hand. So ace king suited will be denoted as AKs. Hands without the "s" will be assumed to be unsuited.

"x" will refer to any card. So Axs would mean an ace with any other card of the same suit as the ace. So if I recommend

playing Axs in a certain position then you would play any suited ace in that spot, regardless of the second card.

Third, I will add a pot-odds chart in the appendix of this book. The chart is self-explanatory and was included to help those of you who are not mathematically inclined. To win at poker does require a little bit of math knowledge, but I assure you that it is nothing too complex. A little bit of memorization and some simple division will be sufficient to beat most games, so if you aren't a math person don't worry too much about it.

Please note that this book contains not only Texas Hold'em concepts, but also basic concepts that are applicable to all poker games. My intention was to make this a complete book, so that it is all you need to read in order to become a winning Hold'em player. If you already understand these concepts (like pot odds) then feel free to skip the chapter. But rereading something you already know never hurt anybody, so don't be afraid to gloss over them. You might pick up something new or relearn something you have forgotten.

Most importantly, I must mention that this book does not attempt to give you concrete answers to every question that will arise at a poker table. There are far too many different scenarios for that to be feasible. According to some scientific estimates the number of atoms in the universe is smaller than the number of ways a 52-card deck can be arranged, so it is easy to see that I can't give you instructions for every situation you will ever face.

What I can and will do is arm you with winning concepts.

These will be your arsenal to use on the green-felt battlefield. Study, practice, and review will teach you how to best use these weapons. There is no easy path to poker mastery, and reading a book—no matter how great it is—isn't going to have you beating the $15/$30 games immediately. Should you come across a book that promises you that, do yourself a favor and leave it on the shelf. If you want to be a winning poker player, you are going to have to read the best poker books (this one especially) and play a lot of hours. You should review hands after they happen and look for ways you could have played them better. The best poker players in the world never play a day without making a mistake, and you will make plenty. Analyze them and learn from them, and the next time a similar situation comes up you will not make the same mistake again.

The good news is that technology and the number of new poker players today make becoming a winning player easier than ever. You can now play very low buy-in games on the Internet, and you can save hand histories for review later. There are a number of software tools you can use to help analyze your play as well. Please see my website at www.mattmaroon.com for more details on these.

When I first started playing poker, Internet card rooms did not exist. The lowest buy in games I had available were local $3/$6 games at seedy bingo halls in the area, which were quite expensive back when I was a broke college student. I was pretty smart about the whole deal and read a couple of the best books available at the time before playing, but still I

was not able to play very well and was lucky to have a few big wins in the beginning. Of course, I promptly lost it all and then some, and I certainly went broke many times, but had I not won at first, I wonder if I ever would have had the courage to continue learning.

Had I had access to the $1/$2 games on the Internet that are available now, I probably would have been able to play more and learn faster, and even if I took a few losses at first, I could have kept playing. Thanks to these low-limit games, poker is no longer inaccessible to people with little money, as even a $25 deposit is more than enough to cut your teeth in some of the micro-limit games spread around the Internet, where the bets are as low as a penny. They even have play money games for those who don't quite understand how the betting system works or need practice reading hands.

I am confident that with this book and lots of practice, anyone of any financial means can become a winning player. The concepts outlined in this book will give you all you need to jump right into the poker games in your local card room or on the Internet. And as you advance, rereading this book will continue to help you learn to beat games of higher and higher limits. Always keep studying, always keep playing, and always keep reviewing your sessions, and before you know it you will have a very profitable hobby. Or maybe even a new profession.

SECTION I

How the Game Is Played

"How long does it take to learn poker, Dad?"
"All your life, son."
—Michael Pertwee

Texas Hold'em is one of the easiest forms of poker to learn and one of the hardest to master. If you have never played any poker at all before, you have chosen a great game. The rules can be learned quickly, yet you can spend the rest of your life studying the game's finer points. You don't need years of practice to become a winning player (though it certainly never hurt anyone), but you will learn something every time you play it for the rest of your life.

Hold'em is a seven card poker game, much like seven card stud, in which you seek to make the best possible five card hand. You receive two cards known as hole cards which are unique to your hand and unseen by your opponents. Then five cards are placed in the middle which are called board cards and are shared by everyone. The player with the best five card hand, using any combination of their hole cards and the board cards, wins the pot.

In Hold'em there are four betting rounds, also known as "streets." The first one, commonly called preflop, comes after each player is dealt their two hole cards. After the first betting round comes the flop, in which three board cards are placed face up in the middle of the table, followed by a betting round. After the flop betting round is complete comes the turn, or fourth street, in which one more card is added to the board, followed by the turn betting round. The last betting round is called the river, or fifth street, in which the fifth board card is placed on the table, followed by the fourth and final betting round. After that betting round, all players left in the pot show their hands and the player with the strongest five-card hand wins the pot.

The Betting Rounds

To determine who has to act first in a hand of Hold'em a dealer button is used. This is a large plastic puck that is usually white and says "dealer" on it. Most games of Hold'em today are dealt by a professional dealer (or a virtual one if on the Internet) so this button symbolizes who would be dealing the hand if it were a self-dealt game. The button always flows clockwise around the table, moving one seat to the left after every hand. Betting in Hold'em also moves clockwise around the table, starting with the player to the left of the button.

When it comes your turn to bet, you have a few different options depending on whether or not anyone has yet bet. If nobody has yet bet then you can either check or bet. Checking means you are going to stay in the hand but not invest any money to do so. Betting means you are going to

put some money into the pot; if you bet $10, then your opponents have to put in at least $10 to remain in the pot. You could legally fold, but you never should do so if you could check instead. Folding means you are throwing your hand away and are giving up any opportunity to win the pot. Be advised, however, that folding when there has not yet been a bet is always a bad play and is generally considered bad etiquette as well. It doesn't cost any more to check than it does to fold, but at least by checking you can try to improve your hand to win the pot later.

If someone has bet, then you have three options: fold, call, or raise. Folding lets you escape the hand with no more investment, but you also give up any chance of winning. Calling means you will match the amount of the bet, so if the bettor bet $10 and you wish to call you must put $10 into the pot as well. Raising means that you are going to put more money into the pot than the bettor, causing everyone else to have to put more money into the pot to remain in the hand; there is usually a limit of three raises per round. So if the original bettor bet $10 and you raise it to $20, then everyone has to put in a total of $20 on that round to stay in the pot.

Every person in a betting round must put in the same amount of money to remain in the hand, unless they are going all in (which we will talk more about in a bit). So if the initial bet is $10, and it is raised to $20 then anyone who wishes to remain in the hand must put a total of $20 in on this round. If they have already called $10 and it is raised to $20 then they need only put in $10 more to call.

A betting round ends when either all players have checked or all players have matched the current bet. The bet keeps moving clockwise around the table until this occurs. Once everyone checks or everyone has put the amount of the current bet in the pot, the round ends and the next one begins.

For an example, let's walk through a flop betting round with four players, A, B, C, and D, who are seated in that order. The betting begins with player A who can check or bet; let's say he checks. Player B can now check or bet. He decides to bet $10. Now play continues around the table clockwise until everyone has called $10. Player C can now fold and put nothing into the pot, call and put $10 into the pot, or raise and put more than $10 into the pot. Let's say he calls, so now it is player D's turn. Player D has the same options as player C, fold, call, or raise, and let's suppose he opts to raise the bet to $20. Now the bet is $20 so we must continue until everyone has either folded or put in $20. The action now comes back to player A, who has so far invested nothing in this round of betting. His options are to call, which would cost him $20 since player D raised the bet to that much, raise the bet to something higher than $20, or fold. Let's say for this example that he decides to fold, so now only players B, C, and D are remaining in the hand.

The action now is on player B, who has already put in $10 that he bet initially. His options are to call $10 more (to match the $20 investment), to raise the bet, or to fold. Let's suppose he calls $10 more. Now the action is on player C, who also has already put in $10, so he has the same options

as player B, and let's suppose he opts to call as well. Now all remaining players have put in the same amount ($20) so the betting round is over. The turn card will now be dealt and a new betting round will begin with players B, C, and D, since A folded and is out of the hand.

Betting Structure

There are many different types of betting structures used in Hold'em, but the three most common are limit, no-limit, and pot-limit. Limit is the most common structure for live action play. In limit poker the amount of the bets is fixed. A typical structure for Hold'em fixes the bet on the last two rounds at twice the size of the bet on the first two rounds. So in a $10/$20 game the bets and raises preflop and on the flop are $10; on the turn and river they are $20.

In no-limit Hold'em bets and raises can be as much as a player wants at any given time, though there is usually a minimum. The only rule is that you must raise an amount equal to or greater than the last bet or raise unless you are going all-in, so if someone bets $50 you must raise it at least $50 more to $100.

Pot-limit is similar to no-limit except the maximum amount you may bet at any one time is equal to the size of the pot. So if there is $50 in the pot you can bet $50. The point of this is to stop opponents from going all-in, forcing them to make more decisions. A lot of experts think that pot-limit is a much tougher game than no-limit because of this.

Table Stakes

One of the most important advances in poker was the advent of table stakes. What that means is that only money that a player has sitting on the table can be used in a pot, and that players cannot be forced out of a hand due to not having enough money. If someone bets $100 and all you have is $50 you can go all-in, but you will only get action on your $50. The other player will get to take his remaining $50 back, or if there are other players who put $100 in, then $50 from each of them will go into a side pot which only they can win. The player who goes all-in for $50 can only win $50 from each of his opponents.

Without table stakes Bill Gates would be the best poker player in the world, as he could simply bet $50 billion into every pot and everyone else would have to fold. This is why in old Westerns you might see cowboys calling bets with the deed to their homes. They had to because otherwise they would lose the pot and everything they had already invested in it even if they had the best hand. Without table stakes the game could never have developed the mass appeal it has today.

Be advised that when playing in a card room that they may have different rules about what can and cannot play on the table. Some will allow only money that has been converted into chips to play while some will allow both chips and bills to play. Some might allow bills but only $100s (this is fairly

common) so if you aren't sure what plays and what doesn't then be sure to ask the dealer or simply convert it all into chips. Chips always play, though even then ones of certain denominations might not. Many card rooms have a rule that one dollar chips don't play when going all-in. It is always good to be aware of such rules before you sit at the table.

The Antes

In every well designed poker game there is some form of ante. An ante is a forced bet to jump start the action. If there were no antes a player would never have any incentive to enter a pot without the best possible hand because there is no penalty for waiting for it. However in a game like Hold'em where the best possible hand only comes around less than once every 200 hands, the antes force you to play more hands because you would ante away all of your money waiting for those aces.

All poker games can be played with many different forms of antes but there is one most commonly accepted type of ante in Hold'em called the blind bet. This happens before any cards are dealt. The player to the left of the button is forced to bet, usually an amount equal to 1/2 or 2/3 of the bet on the first round. This is called the small blind and it is a live bet, meaning that it counts towards the money that player has to put in to see the flop.

After the small blind comes the big blind, which is usually a forced bet equal to the amount of the bet on the first round. This is also a live blind, so if nobody raises the big blind can see the flop for free. The big blind also has the option to raise if nobody else does. This ability to raise by the big blind is called his "option," so if a dealer says "your option," he is asking if you would like to raise.

As an example, let's take a typical $10/$20 game. After every hand the dealer button is pushed left one spot. The player to his left would post 1/2 of the first round bet, or $5. The player after him (the big blind) would post $10. That $10 counts as a bet, so all remaining players must put in at least $10 to see the flop.

Now if nobody raises before the action comes to the small blind (leaving the bet at $10) he can either fold, call the remaining $5, or raise the bet to $20 total by putting $15 more in the pot. If nobody raises before the action comes to the big blind he can either check (and see the flop for free) or raise it to $20.

Winning a Hand

There are two ways to win a hand of Texas Hold'em. The first way is to make all of your opponents fold. You can do this on any round of betting. The second way is to show down the best hand on the river. To do that you will need to know the relative strength of each hand, so here is a list of the hand rankings from strongest to weakest:

Straight Flush: Five cards of consecutive ranks, all of the same suit. In poker games where it is possible for two players to have straight flushes of different suits they are relevant, in

Hold'em they are not. In the event that two players have different straight flushes the higher one wins. The highest straight flush is, of course, the famed royal flush which features 10 through ace of the same suit. An example of a straight flush would be:

Four of a Kind: Four cards of the same rank; suits are irrelevant. In the event that two players have four-of-a-kind, the hand with the higher kicker wins. An example would be:

Full House: Three cards of one rank and two cards of another; suits are irrelevant. An example of a full house would be:

If two players have full houses then the player with the three of a kind with the higher rank wins the pot. So the above full house (which would be termed queens full of eights) is a better hand than jacks full of eights, which looks like:

If two players have a full house where the three of a kind is of the same rank then the hand with the higher pair wins. So queens full of eights would beat queens full of sevens.

Flush: Five cards of the same suit. An example of a flush would be:

If two players have a flush then the one with the highest cards wins. If the both have the same top card (say two players had different ace high flushes) then the next card would decide it, and so on and so forth. It is not possible in Hold'em for two people to have flushes of different suits.

Straight: Five cards of consecutive rank but not all of the same suit. An example would be:

If two players have a straight, then the straight with the highest card wins. So a jack-high straight would beat a 10-high straight.

Three of a Kind: Three cards of the same rank. An example would be:

If two players have three of a kind then the player whose three are of a higher rank wins. If they both have three of the same rank, then the hand with the higher two extra cards (known as kickers) win. So the above hand, trip 7's with a king-jack kicker would beat a hand like:

which would be called trip 7's with a jack-ten kicker.

Two Pair: A hand with two separate pairs and a fifth unpaired card. Example:

If two players both have two pair then the player with the highest top pair wins. So nines and fives would beat eights and sevens. If they have the same top pair then the player with the highest bottom pair wins. So queens and fives would beat queens and fours. And if both of their pairs are the same

then the player with the highest unpaired card (kicker) wins. So jacks and nines with an ace kicker would beat jacks and nines with a queen kicker.

One Pair: Two cards of the same rank with three unpaired cards. An example of a pair would be:

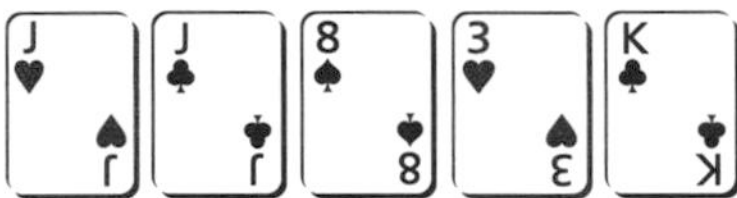

If two players have different pairs then the one of a higher rank wins. If they have the same pair then the hand with the highest kickers wins.

No Pair: Five cards of different ranks that aren't a flush or a straight. The player with the highest unique card wins.

And there you have it. If you are brand new to poker, you are probably thinking it is a bit complicated, but after one day of playing you will remember it. I highly recommend playing poker at one of the play money sites online to get the hang of how the betting rounds work. So now you know how the game is played. Let's see how to play it well.

Mathematical Expectation

One might as well attempt to grasp the game of poker entirely by the use of the mathematics of probability.
—Vannevar Bush

Poker is a very mathematical game. To be a winning player you do not need a degree in statistics, but you are going to have to understand a few basic concepts and be able to apply them. Luckily the most math you will have to do at the table is a little bit of division or addition, so this shouldn't prohibit you from becoming an excellent player. The first math concept we will cover is mathematical expectation, as it is the basis for every decision you will make when playing poker.

Mathematical expectation or expected value (EV), is defined as:

The sum of the values of a random variable with each value multiplied by its probability of occurrence. (Merriam-Webster)

We can express this with the equation:

EV = ((PW) * (AW) – (PL) * (AL)) where
PW = the probability of winning
AW = the amount won

PL = the probability of losing
AL = the amount lost

To simplify this let's apply it to gambling. Your friend offers to flip a coin, and if it lands on heads you will owe him \$5, but if it lands on tails he will owe you \$5. Your mathematical expectation for one coin flip would be the sum of each possible result (+\$5 and -\$5) multiplied by the chance of its occurrence, which in this case is 50 percent. So our expected value in this instance is:

EV = (0.5 * \$5) – (0.5 * \$5)
EV = \$2.5 – \$2.5
EV = \$0

Thus the amount we expect to profit, on average, by flipping coins is exactly \$0. This is what we call an even money wager. On any random flip you might win \$5 or lose \$5, but on average you will not make or lose anything.

Now let's suppose your same friend offered to pay you \$10 if tails lands, but you still only owe him \$5 if it comes up heads. This changes your EV significantly. Our new EV is:

EV = (0.5 * \$10) – (0.5 * \$5)
EV = \$5 – \$2.5
EV = \$2.5

Now let's apply this to poker. Suppose that, with one card to come in a game of Texas Hold'em, and your opponent bets all-in for \$20 into a pot that was \$80 before he bet. You have:

and the board is:

and you are sure your opponent has two pair, 8's and 9's. You now have nine cards left in the deck (any club) that will win the pot for you. You know the two cards in your hand, the two cards in your opponent's hand (an 8 and a 9) and the four cards on the board, which leaves forty-four cards of the fifty-two card deck unknown. Let's compute your EV for calling:

EV = ((PW) * (AW) – (PL) * (AL))
PW = 9/44 (9 clubs out of 44 cards left)
AW = $100 ($80 in the pot plus the $20 your opponent bet)
PL = 35/44 (every card that is not a club)
AL = $20 (the amount you must call, which you will lose if you do not hit a flush)
EV = ((9/44) * $100) – ((35/44) * $20)
EV = $20.45 – $15.91
EV = $4.54

Thus we see that we have a positive expected value of $4.54 dollars, making a call a profitable play. So we would call.

A winning player is one who consistently makes the

plays with highest possible EV. Often the highest possible EV is $0, which means folding, because all other plays have a negative expectation. In the first coin flipping example, where your EV was $0, you would have the same EV by simply not playing. In the second coin flipping example, where your EV was $2.50 (and therefore your friend's EV was -$2.50) your friend would have been better off choosing not to play, since a $0 EV is better than a negative one.

In the coin flipping scenario, much like poker, we are playing a zero-sum game, where every cent that we win has to be lost by someone else. So in the scenario where you have a positive EV, your opponent must have a negative EV of the same magnitude. Thus your friend, in choosing to play that particular game with you, is making a mistake and you are profiting from it. In poker your profit comes from your opponents' mistakes, just like your profit in the coin flipping example came from your friend's mistake. So one way to increase our EV would be to trick our opponents into making plays with a lower EV. There are many ways to accomplish this, the most well-known being the bluff, and we will cover these later.

Sometimes more than one play has a positive EV, perhaps calling versus raising, and a winning player strives to make the play with the higher EV. Of course figuring out your EV is rarely as cut and dried as the above example; if it were, everyone would be an expert poker player. But I will strive throughout this book to teach you to maximize your EV on

every decision you have to make. Poker is a game of incomplete knowledge, and we are rarely fortunate enough to see our opponent's hands, but there are many things we can do to consistently make winning plays.

If the above mathematics seem a bit too complicated to deal with at the table, don't worry. There is a much simpler way to figure out whether a play has a positive or negative EV, which I will detail in the section on pot odds. As I promised, I will reduce the math to a very simple process which you can use while at the table. The purpose of this chapter was merely to explain the underlying theory of positive mathematical expectation that will form the basis for all of your decisions at the poker table—and perhaps in many other areas of your life as well.

Fluctuations and Luck

I must complain the cards are ill shuffled
till I have a good hand.
—Jonathan Swift

In poker, as in other forms of gambling, luck is a key factor. This is important to remember because poker can often be deceptive. The plays with the highest possible EV often blow up in our faces and cost us money, and to the uninformed they might appear to have been incorrect. Perhaps you call with a flush draw and miss, thus costing you a few bets. Or maybe you raise top pair a few times against somebody who is drawing to very few outs (like an inside straight) and that person then catches a miracle river and takes a big pot from you. It might be tempting to think, "Maybe next time I shouldn't raise in that situation," because it would certainly save you money those few times your opponent gets lucky. But you must not let yourself fall for this misguided logic, and you must always strive to make the plays that have the highest EV.

This is why you often hear people speak of the "long run" in poker, and this is the best way to look at every decision you have to make. Ignore short-term fluctuations; they

are an illusion. If an opponent calls a raise with a terrible hand such as 72 offsuit (often referred to as the worst hand in Texas Hold'em), he will certainly get lucky sometimes and win a nice pot. Any starting hand in Hold'em can beat any other hand. But in the long run, if your opponent consistently calls raises with hands like that it will cost him loads of money. For one hand, one day, or maybe even one month his bad calls might work out, but in the end he will surely find himself broke while the players who fold those bad hands take his money.

The long run in poker can sometimes be a very long time. An excellent player can lose for weeks while a terrible player wins night after night. Thus, you must not let losing hands, losing nights, or even losing weeks upset you; they are a natural part of the game. You must think of each game as just one part of a never-ending session. Your ultimate goal is to sit there and play profitable poker night after night, always maximizing your expectation. If the cards go sour for a time you will lose, and there is nothing to be done about it.

Tilting

You must avoid tilting. Tilting (also called steaming) is when a player gets upset about his or her perceived bad luck and proceeds to play very badly. You will see this often in your poker career and even experience it yourself. You will know it when it happens, though you may not admit it and keep playing. It feels like someone lit a match to your stomach. You start playing every hand and taking them all too far. Or you don't play aggressively enough because you fear another loss. I have seen so many world-class players go on tilt and become worse than the average $3/$6 player.

Everyone tilts sometimes. If they tell you that they don't, they are lying. Even the best players in the world tilt occasionally and lose loads of money. What good does being capable of playing excellent poker do if you don't actually do it? When short-term fluctuations get to you, and eventually they will, you must calm yourself down. Get up from the table for a while, take a walk, listen to some music, or just quit playing altogether. When you have lost the capacity to sit there and make good decisions, you must not let yourself play. There will always be a game tomorrow, so come back when you are emotionally stable once again and can continue to play well.

Often when the cards go bad it helps to remember that those same terrible plays your opponents made when they got lucky and beat you are the ones from which you make all of your profit. As I mentioned earlier, poker is what is known as a zero-sum game, which means that for every dollar one player wins, another player must lose one. In fact, if you are playing in a raked game (and most games worth playing in will be raked) then all of the players combined have to lose an amount equal to the rake, making the average player a loser. Thus you need opponents to make mistakes, because if everyone played perfectly everyone would lose. So while bad players may occasionally get lucky and beat you

fight the urge to berate them or to teach them to play better. Without their bad play you couldn't win in the long run.

Remember that if it were not for their lucky nights they would never come back, and the games would dry up quickly. The good players would win every time and the bad players would never come back. Most poker players lose in the long run and play for enjoyment. The few nights where they win are fun enough to keep them coming back for the many nights where they don't, and you want that. It is well worth dealing with those fluctuations, because it means you will always have a good game to come back to.

Avoid Results-Oriented Thinking

You must avoid a very common logical fallacy, which is that if a play worked, then it must have been correct. As I said before, even the worst hands will sometimes beat the best ones. Sometimes 72 will hit two pair and beat pocket aces. But in the long run the better hand will be the winner at the expense of the worse one. So if someone makes a bad play (and this applies even to you) and wins the pot anyway just chalk it up to the natural fluctuations inherent in the game. Conversely if you make a good play and it loses don't simply assume that you did something wrong. Remember to look at each play's EV and only its EV, and ignore short-term results.

The same can be said of an entire session, or even a group of sessions. The fact that you lost does not mean you played badly, and the fact that you won does not mean you played well. The same applies to your opponents. Often you

will play your A game all night long and lose while someone who is calling down with every single hand will win. Do not let this influence your play. Never let yourself utter the cliché "the good cards aren't winning so I decided to play the bad ones," which is the mark of a sucker.

Pot Odds

The secret to all gambling is to identify a good bet. A good bet is when your expectation is positive, or put another way, when the return (assuming you win) is higher than the odds (that is, the inverse of the probability of winning minus one) multiplied by the amount of money bet. As obvious as this seems, many people don't apply it correctly.

—Mason Malmuth

As I mentioned before, there is a simple way to figure out whether or not a play has a positive expectation. You simply check to see if the pot odds are greater than the odds against your winning the hand. Pot odds are the ratio of the amount in the pot to the amount you must put in. For instance if your opponent bets $10 into a $40 pot (making a total of $50 in the pot), your pot odds are $50-to-$10, or 5-1.

First let me briefly describe a little of the terminology we will use here. Odds can either be expressed as against or for something. If a draw has a one in three shot of coming we say the odds against it are two to one, because out of every three times it will miss twice and hit once. Now suppose the same draw has a 2/3 shot of coming. The odds are now two to one for hitting, because out of every three attempts the draw will come twice and miss once.

I said earlier that a play has a positive EV if the pot odds are greater than the odds against your winning the hand. To give an example, let's suppose that you are playing $10/$20 Texas Hold'em and your opponent bet $20 at you on the turn, into a pot that was already $60. You have J♥ 8♥ and the board on the turn reads Q♥ 9♥ 6♠ 5♠. Your opponent bets at you and you have to decide whether to continue with the hand. We will assume that either a heart for a flush or a 10 for a straight will win you the pot. Furthermore, let's say you only have $20 left in front of you, so if you call you will be all-in and there will be no more betting left in the hand, so we can ignore betting on the river. How can you tell whether or not calling would have a positive expectation?

First you compute your pot odds, which are $80-to-$20, which you then reduce to 4-1. Next you calculate the odds against hitting, which are simply the number of cards that don't complete our hand (any card that is not a heart or a 10), compared to the number of cards that do help your hand, also known as "outs." There are nine hearts left in the deck and three tens that aren't a heart (the ten of hearts cannot be counted twice), so you have twelve cards that make your hand. There are four cards you know on the board and two in your hand, leaving forty-six unknown cards. Thus there are 34 cards (46 unknown minus the 12 helpers) that miss your hand and 12 cards that hit, making the odds against your hand 34-12, which you will simplify to 3-1.

So the pot odds (4-1) are greater than the odds against hitting your hand (3-1) meaning that calling has a positive EV and is therefore the correct play. If, in the same situation,

you were getting pot odds of 2-1 your EV would be negative (because the pot odds are less than the odds against hitting), and folding would be the correct play. Remember that folding always has an EV of $0, since you are guaranteed to make $0 and to lose $0 as well, so any play with a positive EV must be better than folding and any play with a negative EV must be worse.

If all of this still seems a bit too complicated I will further simplify it by providing a table of odds (see the appendix) against making hands with various outs with both one and two cards to come. Memorizing some of the basic odds, such as with four outs (an inside straight, or "gutshot"), five outs, eight outs (an open end straight draw), nine outs (a flush draw), and twelve outs (a flush draw and a gutshot) will cover you in nearly all situations. Thus, you need only compare the pot odds to the odds you have memorized, greatly reducing the amount of math you will need to do at the table.

Also note that pot odds apply to many situations other than drawing. Suppose an opponent bets $20 into an $80 pot on the river and you have a weak holding, perhaps middle pair with no kicker. Because you don't know your opponent's cards, you can't say for sure whether you have the best hand. You think that there is a 25 percent chance he is bluffing and that you have the best hand. Should you call? Again pot odds are useful.

Your odds here are $100-to-$20, or 5-1. Because you think your opponent has a 25 percent chance of being on a bluff here, the odds against your opponent bluffing are 75-

to-25, or 3-to-1. Since the pot odds (5-1) are greater than the odds against your hand being the best, calling has a positive expectation. If in the same situation you thought there was only a 15 percent chance your opponent was bluffing, then the odds against him bluffing would be 85-15, or 5.67-to-1. In this case your pot odds (5-to-1) are smaller than the odds against your hand winning (5.67-to-1) so a fold would be the play with the highest EV.

Pot odds can also be used for determining whether to bluff. Suppose you are playing $3/$6, and a pot contains $60 on the river. You are sure your hand is not the best and are deciding whether to bet $6 on a bluff. How often must your bluff succeed to have a positive expectation? This is relatively simple to figure out. When your bluff works you make $60 and when it fails you lose $6, so the pot is laying you 10-1 odds. That means that if the chance of winning the pot is less than 10-1 against, your bluff has a positive EV. To put that another way your bluff must succeed one out of every eleven times to be profitable. If you had only one opponent left and your betting on prior streets might have given your opponent good reason to believe you actually had a hand, you might venture a bluff here because it doesn't have to succeed very often to be profitable.

Please note that we do not factor any money we have already put into the pot into the equation any differently than we would money that has been put into the pot by an opponent. Once money is out of your hands it ceases to be yours and belongs to the pot. Do not ever remain in a pot because you have already put money in it. Bad players often do this, and people refer to it as "chasing bad money with good." A $100 pot is a $100 pot—whether you put in $5 or $50 of it makes no difference to your EV. Whether the money in the pot came from you, from your opponents, or fell from heaven (or any combination thereof) is immaterial; all that matters is how much is there.

Implied Odds

In our above poker examples we assumed that we were all-in so that we could ignore betting on later rounds. In the real world of poker, however, most decisions are not as simple as all-in or fold. Usually you will have plenty of chips left after the flop or the turn, and thus you must factor betting on later streets into your equations. This is called implied odds.

Implied odds can work either for or against you. For instance if you call with a flush draw on the turn and the river misses you chances are you won't put in any more bets, so you will lose the same amount you would have if you were all-in, one turn bet. If you hit your flush on the river though you will probably bet or raise, thus increasing the implied odds you are receiving on the turn.

Here is an example of how implied odds work for you. You are playing $10/$20 Texas Hold'em. The pot on the turn is $50 and your opponent bets $20 at you. You hold 23 and the board is AK96. You are pretty sure your opponent has a good hand, maybe something like a pair of aces with a good kicker. This leaves you 9 outs, with 46 unknown cards, meaning your odds against hitting are 37-to-9, or roughly 4.11-to-1. Your pot-odds on the turn are only 3.5-1 however, which would indicate that you should fold. But your implied odds here indicate a call.

If the river is a heart you figure to get at least one more bet ($20) out of your opponent on the river, making your implied odds $90-to-$20, or 4.5-to-1, which is greater than the 4.11-to-1 odds against your hitting. If your opponent has a very strong hand, like two pair or a set (maybe he hit two pair or three of a kind with the same card that gave you your flush) he might even bet the river and you can raise, netting an extra $40. Of course if he has two pair or a set on the turn then one or two of your flush outs might give him a full house and cost you as much as $60, but we will assume for purposes of this chapter that the times you hit and win $40 will even out with the times you hit and lose $40 or more, and assume that if your flush comes you will win, on average, one big bet from it. Thus our implied odds now instruct us to call.

Whereas implied odds worked for you in the above example they worked against your opponent, and they will sometimes work against you too. Suppose you have the made hand on the turn and your opponent has the drawing hand. Now implied odds are working against you. Your opponent with the drawing hand can bet or raise the river if he hits, but can easily fold if he misses, losing nothing more. Of course the money in the pot often gives both of you correct odds to continue on. In that case the best thing you

can do is give your opponent the worst odds possible by betting the turn, which we will cover in later chapters.

Implied odds can also work against you when there are two cards to come. Suppose you have a gutshot straight draw after the flop. You would need roughly 5-to-1 odds to make a call profitable if the decision were all-in or fold. But what if you and your opponent both have plenty of chips remaining? In that case you will often have to call a bet on the turn on the hands where you miss, thus reducing your implied odds. Here's why:

Let's say you are playing $5/$10 and your opponent bets $5 into a $25 pot at you on the flop and you have a gutshot (four outs). If you look in the appendix, you will see that you are now roughly 5-to-1 against hitting with two cards to come and you are now getting 6-to-1 pot odds, an easy call if you are all-in and implied odds aren't a factor. But let's assume that both you and your opponent both have plenty of chips and see how this changes matters.

When you miss the turn your opponent will bet and you will have to call $10. This means that on the hands you lose you will lose $15 ($5 on the flop and $10 on the turn). We will assume that on the hands you win you get one bet on every street from your opponent, meaning that on the hands you win you get $50 ($30 in the pot on the flop, and $10 on each of the next two streets). This means your implied pot-odds are now only $50-to-$15, or roughly 3.33-to-1, which is far lower than the odds against hitting (5-to-1) making the decision an easy fold. Even if you assume you will get to raise one of the big bets if you hit and get called your odds are still only \$60-to-\$15, or 4-to-1, making a call still unprofitable.

Remember that poker is a game of incomplete information. You usually don't know what your opponent has, and you don't know how he will react to your actions. With experience you will learn to read your opponents' hands and come to understand how they will react to many different situations, which will help you determine your implied odds. When you are first starting out you would probably be best advised to pay attention to your direct pot odds most of the time. If a draw doesn't have the odds required to take a card off, don't do it. Chances are that even if your implied odds make the draw profitable you won't be losing much by folding.

But as you advance try to think more of your implied odds and less of your direct odds. Try to gauge what your opponent has, how likely he is to bet the turn or to pay you off if you raise. Ability to accurately judge your implied odds and then act on them is a significant portion of what separates winners from losers. As you gain more experience the math of poker will become intuitive and you will not think about it any more than you think about breathing or blinking your eyes, but as a beginner it will be of great help to review hands afterward and calculate both your direct odds and your implied odds as well as you can.

Betting

The only thing that interferes with my learning is my education.
—ALBERT EINSTEIN

Poker is a very counterintuitive game. Most of what we learn in life tells us to go about life in a rather passive manner. It is a natural human tendency to try to achieve our goals while investing as little time, money, or effort as possible. Evolutionary psychologists believe this has been ingrained in man since our earliest days. Our nine to five culture teaches us to go through life meekly, taking what comes our way. This passive behavior must be overcome by anyone who wants to become a winning poker player.

The only way to go about winning games of even the lowest stakes is to become an aggressive player. Aggressive players are the ones who are constantly doing everything in their power to increase their chances of winning pots. They are the ones who bet and raise frequently, knocking as many people out of the pots as they can and charging the rest a heavy price to see a showdown. You can't become a winning poker player unless you learn to be aggressive, and in Hold'em that means doing a lot of betting and raising whenever you choose to remain in a hand.

In all forms of poker betting or raising (which is basically the same as betting) can accomplish a wide variety of things. We have to distinguish two different types of betting: betting with cards left to come, and betting when all the cards are out, or river betting. Here is a list of reasons why you might bet or raise with many cards left to come, such as preflop, and on the flop and turn.

Betting with Cards Left to Come

To make opponents fold hands that have the correct odds to draw against you.

If your opponent has a hand that is getting the correct odds to draw at you then he has a positive EV. By making him fold that hand you are stealing that EV from him. Let's say you raise preflop from early position with:

and the big blind defends. The flop comes:

it checks to you, and you bet. Suppose the big blind has a hand like

which gives him ten outs, any queen, jack, or ten. At this point, your opponent is getting 5-1 odds on a roughly 3.5-1 shot (and that is just on the turn) but from his perspective it might appear that he only has four outs (which is what he would have if you had an ace or a king). Thus he might fold (thinking he has something like an 11-1 underdog), which if he knew your hand would be incorrect. So by betting you might make your opponent lay down a hand that has the correct odds to try to beat you. Thus he is throwing away his positive EV and you are receiving it.

To make an opponent fold a better hand than yours. Imagine in the same above example your opponent held:

It may be hard for him to continue on after the flop, given that the majority of your preflop raising hands from early position will either contain an ace or a king, or be a pair bigger than tens. Of course, in this particular instance you are actually a huge underdog and your EV is very small, but if you bet and your opponent folds you win the pot. Note that making your opponent fold the same hand you have is similar, though not as profitable because you are really only stealing half of the pot since half of it belonged to you anyway. Still if you knew your opponent hand the same hand as you, you would undoubtedly do everything you could to force him out.

To reduce an opponent's expectation and therefore increase your own.

This applies to when your opponent is drawing and has the correct odds to do so. Suppose your opponent has a flush draw on the turn and that hitting it is the only way he can beat you, giving him a roughly 1/5 shot (or 4-1 against) of winning the pot. Let's assume we are playing $10/$20 and you and three opponents saw the flop heads up for a raise, making 8 bets in the pot. You bet the pot, the flush draw called, and the rest of the opponents folded putting 10 bets ($100) in the pot. We will also assume that if your opponent makes his flush you will pay him one bet on the river, and if he misses he will not pay you anything. Let's calculate what his expectation would be if you bet the turn and what it would be if you didn't.

Opponent's EV when you do bet the turn

EV = ((PW) * (AW) – (PL) * (AL)) where

PW = 0.2

AW = $140 ($100 in the pot after the flop, and $20 from you on both the turn and river)

PL = 0.8

AL = ($20)

EV = (0.2 * 140 – 0.8 * 20)

EV = 28–16

EV = 12

Opponent's EV when you don't bet the turn

EV = ((PW) * (AW) – (PL) * (AL)) where

PW = 0.2

AW = $120 ($100 in the pot after the flop, and $20 from you on the river)

PL = 0.8

AL = $0

EV = (0.2 * 120 – 0.8 * 0)

EV = 24 – 0

EV = 24

So we can see pretty easily that by you not betting the turn your opponent is making $12 more in the long run than he would if you bet the turn. Note that he is quite correct in calling your turn bet, but he makes more profit in the long run by getting that river card for free. Of course this is a zero sum game, so his $12 profit has to be your $12 loss, but just to prove it we will examine your EV in both cases.

Your EV when you do bet the turn

EV = ((PW) * (AW) – (PL) * (AL)) where

PW = 0.8

AW = $120 ($100 in the pot after the flop, and $20 from your opponent on the turn)

PL = 0.2

AL = \$40 (your bet on the turn and your call on the river)

EV = (0.8 * 120 – 0.2 * 40)

EV = 96 – 8

EV = 88

Your EV when you don't bet the turn

EV = ((PW) * (AW) – (PL) * (AL)) where

PW = 0.8

AW = \$100 (\$100 in the pot after the flop)

PL = 0.2

AL = \$20 (your call on the river)

EV = (0.8 * 100 – 0.2 * 20)

EV = 80 – 4

EV = 76

So here we see that by not betting on the turn you reduce your EV from \$88 to \$76, the same \$12 difference. Hence betting against a drawing hand, even though that drawing hand is correct to call you, puts extra money in your pocket.

Also, when your opponent does not have the odds to draw at you, betting can give him a negative EV, whereas checking (assuming he is drawing live) gives him a positive EV, however small.

Remember that you always want your opponent to make the play with the worst EV for him. In cases where your opponent's EV for calling becomes negative you actually want him to call, as opposed to cases where you simply reduce your opponent's EV to a lower positive number. If your opponent's EV is positive you would rather your opponent fold, because you would rather him have a zero EV than a small positive one.

Also please note that by a drawing hand I mean any hand that is not the most likely hand to win the pot but still is capable of winning the pot. In any pot there is a best hand (which is the hand most likely to win the pot) and any other hands are drawing hands or simply dead money. Often someone has a hand they think is the best but that is really a drawing hand (or is drawing dead) and sometimes there may be even be a hand that is currently the highest ranked but is less likely to win than another. For instance,

is a higher ranked hand than

on the flop of

but the

will actually win on the turn or river over 70 percent of the time. Thus, the pocket fours is the drawing hand.

To extract money from a hand that is drawing dead.
Anytime a hand is drawing dead and it calls your $20 bet, it is $20 straight in your pocket, assuming it doesn't later steal you off of the hand by bluffing. If your opponent is drawing dead, your entire focus is to make him put as much money in the pot as possible. Conversely if you are drawing dead, you should run for the hills.

To gain information.
This generally shouldn't be the only reason for a bet, but it can be a deciding factor if you are having a tough time deciding between betting and checking. Often, whether an opponent raises or not can help you narrow down the range of hands he might hold. For instance a lot of people I run across always slowplay trips when they flop them, so if I bet on a flop like

and they raise I can be very sure that they don't have a king. Thus if I have a hand like

I can play it fairly strongly and be confident that it is good. Note that I did not bet solely to find out what he had as many of the above reasons for betting were present. And also note that had he just called I still don't know whether he has a king, a spade draw, or maybe something like a lower pair that he thinks might be good.

Also in my example betting only gives me good information because my opponent is fairly predictable. Were I playing against a tough opponent who is capable of raising with a king, a seven, a pocket pair, a spade draw, or perhaps nothing at all (and is also capable of just calling with all of those) my bet would tell me very little. So in general, only factor-in the information against players whose action will actually give you information. And think of it as more of a pleasant side effect than a primary consideration.

To deceive your opponent on a later street.

Often opponents will put you on a hand or exclude some hands from their mental list of your possible holdings when you bet, and if they are wrong that misinformation can be hazardous to them later. For instance suppose you hold a

hand like

and the flop comes

and you lead out into your opponent.He may exclude the possibility of your having a full house because most people would slowplay that so if he catches a straight or flush later he might take it pretty far on one or two of the big bet rounds. However had you check-called the flop, then went nuts on the turn he might be more suspicious of your having slow-played a monster, as that is what many people would do with a hand like KJ there.

Betting early might also help deceive opponents later when bluffing. Whenever you bet you are saying to everyone, "I have a hand." Now they may or may not believe you but if you are saying on the earlier rounds that you have a hand they are going to be more likely to believe you when you say it later. This is part of selling a bluff, which I will talk about more in the chapter on bluffing.

To get a free card.

This is more applicable to raising than betting, though it can apply to both. For instance you have

and the flop comes

You are heads up and your opponent bets. If you raise here and your opponent calls, chances are he is going to check the turn. If the turn is not a spade you now can opt to simply check behind him to get the river card for free to try to make your flush.

Beware though that if your opponent re-raises or three-bets and leads out at you on the turn, you have now lost two small bets by your attempt to steal. Of course this effect is greatly reduced by the fact that you will still hit a flush 1/3 of the time anyway, so even if your opponent three-bets the flop you will still, on average, get two of them back. So it is really only costing you one small bet.

However if your free card attempt succeeds you are saving one small bet because you put in one extra small bet on the flop to avoid putting in one big bet on the turn. Also if you hit the turn you can simply continue betting, and you have now netted an extra small bet on the flop.

Just remember to only try this play when you are in late position, betting last in the round. It can work with any number of opponents, but if any are behind you they can easily pounce when you miss your flush and check the turn. Only do it if you are either guaranteed to be the last player, or if you only have one player behind you who you think will fold to your raise on the flop.

To get more money in the pot.

This is something you want to do any time your hand is more likely to win than the average hand in the pot. Suppose you have the nut flush draw against five opponents on the flop on an unpaired board. Now your hand has a roughly one in three shot of winning, but the average hand with six players has a one in six shot. Now you want to dump as much money in the pot as you possibly can. Suppose the first opponent bets and the rest call. You would want to raise then, as you have a 1/3 shot of winning everything that goes in there, and if your raise sucks in five extra bets (1/3 of which you will win) plus your own you will receive, on average, two bets back. Not bad for a one bet investment.

By the same token if you were the second player to act in a six-handed pot on the flop with the same nut flush draw and the first player bet, you would probably want to simply call and let all of your opponents trail in behind you. You actually stand to get more money in the pot by just calling.

You have no made hand to protect, so nobody is drawing at you, and you probably can't steal the pot with that many opponents so you therefore have no interest in driving people out. Chances are that if your flush comes you will win and if it doesn't come you won't, no matter how many people are in the pot. The odds of stealing the pot are abysmal with that many players in. None of the above conditions for a bet or raise are met, so you would simply call.

Notice that often many or all of the above reasons to bet might be valid. In those cases, it is a strong argument in favor of a bet. In deciding which move to make in poker you must take all of your options and weigh the positives and the negatives inherent in each. Your ability to do this will come from experience and study.

Reasons Not to Bet with Cards Left to Come

Betting, of course, is not always a good idea. There are a number of reasons why it might be better to just check, call, or fold. Here are some reasons why you shouldn't bet:

It decreases your EV.

We saw in an above example that betting on the turn when your opponent had a flush draw decreased his EV. The decrease in his EV is the same whether you bet and he called, or he bet and you called. Who did the betting doesn't matter in terms of expectation, just how much betting there was. So if you have a flush draw on the turn and you don't think you have any chance of stealing the pot and are pretty sure your opponent has a better hand, then you should probably just check because betting will decrease your EV.

It reopens the betting.

Suppose there are four people left in the pot, you and three opponents, and you are last to act. Everyone checks to you. If you bet now all three of your opponents have the opportunity to raise. If you check, however, the betting for that round is closed, there can be no more, and the next card (or showdown after the river) will be guaranteed. This is of consideration only when you are last to act (or if you are somehow certain that everyone behind you will check) as otherwise the betting is still open.

You might be better off inducing a bluff. I will cover bluff inducing more in a later chapter, but many times you will find that betting might scare an opponent out of the pot, whereas checking to him might entice him to bet a hand that isn't worth it. Thus you are extracting a bet out of him. Also if you are wrong and he has a better hand than yours you might be saving some bets.

You might be better off slowplaying.

Sometimes when you have something like

and the flop hits:

You might want to consider not betting and trying to let your opponents hit something big. You have the pot pretty much locked up here with your straight flush (at best an opponent could have one out, and anyone even having the higher straight flush draw is unlikely so you may want to consider trying to trap opponents.) If another diamond comes someone with the ace of diamonds will put in a lot of bets before they figure out it isn't good. And even if just something like the:

turns somebody might pick up a straight and put in a few big bets with it later.

I will go into when you should and should not slowplay later, but for the most part I don't recommend it.

So now you have a solid list of reasons for and against betting or raising in different situations. This is by no means meant to be a complete list, and if you think of good reasons while at the table factor them into your decisions as well. Unfortunately in poker we don't have time at the table to compute the exact EV for a number of different scenarios, and even if we did the number of intangibles would make it impossible to go through all of them and figure out the best play. But we can use our experience (the best teacher of all) to whittle it down to the few that are most likely, approximate their value, and go from there.

Betting with All of the Cards Out

Once all of the cards are dealt all of the reasons for betting go out the window. There are no more draws, so the best hand has been determined and will win unless it folds. There are only two possible reasons to bet on the river in Texas Hold'em, and they are to get a worse hand to pay you and to get a better hand to fold.

To get a worse hand than yours to pay you is called value betting. When you bet a hand hoping that an inferior hand will call, you are betting for value. If you succeed you win a big bet. Pretty simple, right?

Actually, figuring out whether or not to value bet is somewhat complex. First you have to decide whether or not you might be better off trying to induce a bluff. If you think your opponent was calling you with a draw the whole way and you are pretty sure that he will simply fold if you bet then you might want to check to him if he acts behind you. Obviously if he checks to you, you will just bet and pray he calls, but unless he has at least ace high he probably won't.

You also have to consider the overlay you are giving your opponent by betting. Let's say that you bet and you intend to call if your opponent raises. Now if you have him beat he can either fold, netting you $0, or just call, netting you 1 big bet. But if he has you beat he might opt to raise in which case you lose two bets. So by value betting you are laying your opponent odds.

Also you should consider check raising on the river as well, but again you are laying your opponent the same odds. Still, it is a consideration because often your opponent may have a hand that is good enough to call your river bet, but not good enough to raise. In this case, he might bet if you check to him and call if you raise. Thus, check raising might net you an extra bet.

The second reason to bet, to get a hand that is better than yours to fold, is called bluffing. Stealing a pot like this is one of the best things that you can do because there are usually many bets involved. If you make a successful value bet and are called you profit by one big bet. But a successful bluff might net you dozens of them.

Of course the size of the pot makes folding the best hand a catastrophe, and most of your opponents know this and therefore will call quite often making bluffing on the river very hard. You should also do the same and be very careful not to fold the best hand on the river, especially when the pot is large. In fact the larger the pot, the more inclined you should be to call. Also the more likely your opponent is to bluff, the more likely you should be to call him.

So there you have the two reasons to bet after all the

cards are dealt. If you are considering a bet on the river, ask yourself, "Can my bet accomplish either of the above goals?" If the answer is no, then don't bet. If the answer is yes you still may be better served by not betting. If you are ever in doubt on the river in limit Hold'em I recommend checking and/or calling, especially if the pot is large. If you are positive your hand is no good, just go ahead and fold, but if you think there is a chance it is good and it will only cost you one bet then give it a shot. If nothing else calling your opponents down with junk a few times will send them the message that you aren't easily bluffed and that might convince them not to bluff at you in the future, which may save you a pot later.

Position

Your position never gives you the right to command.
—Dag Hammarskjold

While the above statement may be true of leadership in life, it is dead wrong when it comes to poker. Your position in the betting sequence is one of the most important poker concepts to understand. It is a factor in most of the decisions you will make at a poker table. In fact you will often throw away hands in early position that you would play or even raise with in late position. That is because being last to act is greatly preferable to being first.

In Hold'em, the betting order for each hand is fixed before the hand is even dealt. One player has the button, usually a small plastic disc, and that player is always the last to act. The player to his left is the first to act and play moves right to left (clockwise) around the table. So the best position to have would be the button. The second best would be to the right of the button (this is often referred to as the cut-off) and so on and so forth, with the worst position being to the left of the button. This may change slightly due to the blinds preflop (who act last there but are forced to post money) but even there the difference is minimal, and on all other betting streets the button is the best position to have.

Advantages of Position

The player who is last to act has many advantages. The first is that he has more information with which to make his decision than anyone else because he has already seen what everyone else has done in the betting round. For instance suppose you hold a hand like 6♦ 7♦ before the flop and you only want to play it if you can see the flop for one bet with a few other limpers. If you are in first position and you limp in with this hand, the betting may be raised and re-raised behind you, or perhaps one player will raise and everyone will fold. But if you hold the same 6♦ 7♦ in last position, you know where the betting stands and how many other players are in the pot. Preflop you still have the blinds to act behind you, but you know that if you limp in on the button there will generally be no raise.

Being in late position has other advantages as well. One is that it gives you much more control over the pot. If everyone checks to you and you decide to check then you get to see the next card (or showdown) for free. If you check in early position, people behind you can still bet. Similarly if you are in last position and the first position player bets, then you can call knowing that there will be no raise. The first position player and all of the other players in the pot have to consider the possibility of a raise coming from behind them if they decide to call, but you do not.

Position can also help you capitalize on your good hands. If you are in early position and you hit a good hand you have to decide whether to bet or to check-raise. If you try to check-raise but nobody behind you bets then you miss a bet. But if you bet and someone calls in a situation where you could have check-raised them you missed a bet as well. If you are in late position your decision is fairly easy—you simply bet or raise.

Combating Position

Unfortunately you aren't going to always be in position during a hand. Oftentimes you are going to find yourself in a situation where one or more opponents have a positional advantage over you. There are a few tools you can use to help counteract their positional advantage.

The first way to combat your opponents' positional advantage is by simply not letting them have any more of it than you have to in the first place. The way to do this is by being selective preflop and trying to limit the number of hands where you are out of position after the flop. You can do this by playing more hands in later position than you do in earlier position, and by raising hands in early position rather than limping. I will talk more about the importance of position in preflop selection in a bit, but for now it is just important to understand that by playing hands in a later position you are gaining an edge in postflop play.

Check-Raising

The second weapon against position is the check-raise. The check raise is simply when a player checks a hand and then raises after an opponent behind them bets. Check-raising is a very important part of Texas Hold'em. If you never check-raise you are giving your opponents too much of a positional advantage.

Suppose the player to your right, who will act before you almost all of the time, always bets his good hands, check-calls his draws, and check-folds his bad ones. If you are in a hand with him your positional advantage is insurmountable because you will always know about what he has. If he bets you know he has a good hand and can fold your weaker holdings. If he checks you can bet anything and know there is a good shot he will fold and no chance he will raise you. And if he calls you can put him on a draw and play accordingly. He is in very bad shape.

Now let's suppose the same opponent starts check-raising a number of his good hands, and maybe some of his draws and just plain bad hands too. You can no longer bet with impunity anytime he checks because you now know that you might get raised. You also no longer know when he checks that he doesn't have a good hand. Some of your positional advantage has been taken away from you. You still have many advantages over him, but if he plays well he can keep that to a minimum. Just the threat of him raising forces you to consider checking behind him, whereas without check-raises you would bet every time.

So you can see that check-raising is a very important part of poker. You will sometimes hear people say that it is dirty or improper, and some people even disallow it in their home games, but without it a good portion of the skill element

of the game is removed. Even the threat of a check-raise, perhaps more than the actual check-raise itself, is necessary to prevent position from becoming an overpowering advantage. In the rare instances where you might come across a game with no check-raising you could beat it easily by simply playing nothing but premium holdings in early position and by playing anything at all in late position.

Relative Position

So far we have been mainly talking about absolute position, which is merely your position relative to the dealer button. The closer to the button you are the better your absolute position is. But there is another type of position to consider which is what I call relative position. Relative position is your position relative to the bettor.

The ideal relative position is the spot immediately to the right of the bettor. This is because you get to see how everyone reacts to the bet and then make your decision. If nobody raises then you can decide whether or not there will be further betting on that round. If you decide to fold or just call then the betting round ends and the next one is guaranteed. If you choose to raise then you can reopen the betting, allowing another player to raise. Let's look at an example.

There are five players in on the flop, players A, B, C, D, and E, who are sitting in that order. Everyone checks to player E who bets. The player with the best relative position is now player D because he gets to wait and see what players A, B, and C do before making his decision. If all of the players call or fold then he can elect to either fold himself or just call. If he just calls the betting round is over and the turn is guaranteed, so he is only risking one bet. If he elects to raise he then reopens the betting for everyone, in which case player C would now have the best relative position.

In the same above example, where it checked around to player E who bet, player A has the worst relative position. If he calls he has to worry about players B, C, and D raising behind him. Even if he raises he has to worry about three-betting. Thus player A might be forced to fold some hands he might have called if he were in player C's spot and could guarantee seeing the turn for only one bet.

It should be easy to see that the more players are in the pot the more important relative position becomes. This is because there are more people who might check-raise. If you are playing a pot heads up relative position is irrelevant. If you are playing a pot with six opponents this can have great influence over your decisions.

Anticipating Relative Position

As you can see relative position can change many times throughout the course of a hand or even an individual betting round. Still there are some ways you can anticipate who will bet, and therefore your relative position, on future rounds. For instance people who raise preflop often bet the flop. And people who see a flop know this so they often check to that player, and if they have a good hand they will often check-raise it. If you are in the seat directly behind (to the left of)

a raiser before the flop, there is a very good chance that you will find yourself with bad relative position after the flop.

This is one of many reasons why you should consider three-betting (re-raising) preflop rather than calling. You really shouldn't be calling many raises preflop, and I will talk much more in depth about this later, but because of your relative position on the flop it is often far better to three-bet preflop and try to drive everyone else out and get the pot down to two people. If the pot is two-handed, then relative position doesn't really matter.

Unfortunately most of learning to anticipate your relative position on future rounds comes from experience and isn't something I can fully teach you here. As you gain experience you will get a feel for how people's actions on one round influence their actions on later rounds, and you will become more adept at using this to your advantage. Always try to remain conscious when reviewing hands of how both your absolute and your relative positions affected or should have affected your play.

SEVEN

Bluffing

You bluffed me! I don't like it when people bluff me.
It makes me question my perception of reality.
—Diane Frolov and Andrew Schneider

Quite possibly, the most romanticized part of poker is the bluff. Betting your opponent off of a winning hand, particularly one with a lot of money in the pot, might seem like the ultimate thrill in poker. And I suppose it is, but in limit poker, where your opponent is often getting odds of 5-1 or greater to call one more bet, it is often very hard to pull off a successful bluff. Trying to bluff too often against opponents who call too much to begin with is just going to cost you extra money in the long run.

Most of the times you are going to run a pure bluff, which I will define as betting with a hand that is not the best hand and has little or no chance of becoming the best hand, you are going to do so with all of the cards out. When deciding whether or not to bluff there are three factors involved which we can use to mathematically determine whether or not it is a good play. They are the size of the pot, the amount you must bet to bluff, and the chances of your opponent folding.

The Mathematics of Bluffing

Calculating the EV of a bluff is fairly straightforward if you know those three variables. The first two are very easy to determine but unfortunately the third, the chances of your opponent folding, is often much harder. This is where good observation comes into play. If you have been watching everything going on at the table, you will have a much better idea of that opponent's tendencies than you would if you have not been paying attention or if you have just sat down. If you know nothing about your opponent then you will simply have to assume he is a typical player and go from there.

As an example let's say we are playing $5/$10 and a pot has $60 in it. You are positive that your opponent has you beat but you think that there is some chance that you can bet him off of his hand. How much chance of that must there be to make him fold?

The easiest way to do that is to compare the odds we are getting against the odds of our opponent folding. In the above example we have to bet $10 to win $60, so our pot odds are 6-1. So our bluff has to be successful more than one out of seven times to be a good play.

So if we have an opponent who is a calling station and you suspect that he will call 9 out of 10 times then it is a bad play. 1 out of 7 is roughly 14 percent of the time, but your bluff will only succeed 10 percent of the time so it is a bad play. We can see that by using the EV equation from earlier:

EV = ((PW) * (AW) – (PL) * (AL)) where
PW = the probability of winning
AW = the amount won
PL = the probability of losing
AL = the amount lost

PW in this case is our chance of our opponent folding (10 percent) and AW is the amount of money in the pot ($60). PL is the probability of our opponent calling (90 percent) and AL is the amount we lose by attempting to bluff, in this case $10. Plug those numbers in and we get:

EV = (0.10 * $60) – (0.90 * $10)
EV = $6 – $9
EV = –$3

So our bluff in this instance has a negative EV of $3. It would be better to check and fold. Now let's suppose we think our opponent will fold one out of five times (20 percent) and compute our EV then.

EV = (0.20 * $60) – (0.90 * $10)
EV = $12 – $9
EV = $3

Now our EV has become a positive $3. So our bluff is a good move, even though 4 out of 5 times it will fail. This is where poker becomes rather subjective, as you must trust your ability to judge your opponents' calling frequencies. It is very easy to attempt a bluff, be successful, and therefore determine that it was a good bet. But notice that even in the first case, where it is mathematically a bad bet, it will still work one time in ten.

By the same token, you can't just assume that a bluff was bad because it didn't work. If you look at the second example we see that the bluff has a positive EV even though it is going to fail 80 percent of the time. So you are just going to have to make the judgment call, go with it, and not let the results fool you.

If you are succeeding with a very high number of your bluffs then you might want to consider that you are overestimating the chances your opponent is going to call and try bluffing a bit more. If a high percentage of your bluffs are working then chances are you aren't bluffing enough. If your bluffs only need to succeed 20 percent of the time to be profitable, but you find that 80 percent of your bluffs succeed, then you are missing a lot of good bluffing opportunities.

Of course, if you find that you are bluffing and getting called the vast majority of the time you might try to consciously adapt your judgment because you could be consistently underestimating the chances of your opponent calling. I am talking over a very large sample here, maybe thousands of hours of playing. If the odds you are getting on the river average out to 6-1 against but only one out of ten of your bluffs are succeeding then you are going to have to be a bit more selective.

When Opponents Bluff

The same laws apply when you are determining whether to call an opponent's bet, which may be a bluff. In that case the numbers are reversed, with the amount won being the amount in the pot plus your opponent's bet and the amount lost being merely your own bet. This means that if you are facing a $10 bet with a $60 pot your call must win only 1 in 7 times to be correct. Anything above that is going to be profitable.

Bluffs only need to succeed a small amount of the time to be correct, so if you find that a high percentage of yours are succeeding you aren't doing it enough. The same is true of river calls. If you only need to be correct 20 percent of the time but are winning 80 percent of the time you call then you are folding a lot of winners. The way to win at limit Hold'em is not by making good laydowns on the river. Save those for the flop and turn.

That is why I suggest that if you are only facing one bet and you don't know what to do you should call. Of course you should adjust that advice according to how your opponents play. If you are up against an opponent who seldom bets the river and always shows a monster when he does, then you should be much less inclined to call him than you would a typical player; the odds of him bluffing (and therefore the PW in our EV equation) are much smaller. And if you are up against a player who seems to bet the river a lot and is often called and forced to roll over garbage, then you should be more inclined to call him.

Proper Bluffing Frequency

As I mentioned above we should adapt how often we call on the river depending on how often our opponents bluff. Your

opponents know this too and will do the same for you. If you never bluff then your opponents know when you are betting that you have a good hand and can play accordingly. They aren't going to pay you off. And if you bluff too much they are going to call you more, thus costing you money and preventing you from making good bluffs in the future.

That is why it is important against observant opponents to bluff just the right amount. Against a perfect opponent in our above example you would want to bluff exactly 1 in 7 times. Then no matter what he does he breaks even. If he calls every time he will win $60 once and lose $10 6 times, for a net of $0.If he folds he will save $10 6 times and win $60 once, also for a net of $0. In any case, assuming that he doesn't have a tell on you enabling him to determine when you are bluffing and when you aren't, he cannot get a positive EV from you.

But at the same time most of your opponents aren't perfect. Maybe they aren't paying attention and don't know how often you bluff. Maybe they are paying attention and don't know how to use the information correctly. In either case it may be best for you to adapt your bluffing frequency to exploit their weaknesses.

For instance if your opponent is a calling station you may want to not bluff at all or be much more selective. If he is going to call you every time then you are going to have a $0 EV by bluffing that 1 in 7 times. But if you instead just value bet the six times that you do have a hand and check the one time you don't then you are netting $60 total, for an EV of $8.5 per hand. $8.5 is much better than $0.

If your opponent folds too often, say 1 in 5 times, you should bluff much more. Of course you don't want to bet every time, as even the weakest opponent will catch on to you and correct their bad habit of folding, but you want to bluff as much as you can without causing him to start calling you more. Exactly how much bluffing you should do will be a judgment call that you will get better at making as you gain experience.

Raise Bluffing

All of the bluffs outlined above were made by betting, but it is possible to bluff with a raise too. If, in the above example, the pot were $50 and your opponent had bet $10 on the river (making it now $60) to bluff you would have to put in $20. Your pot odds would now only be 6-2 (rather than 6-1) so your bluff would have to succeed 2 out of 8 (or 1 in 4) times to be correct. This is almost twice as often.

Furthermore your bluff is much less likely to succeed. Most times an opponent bets the river he will call a raise. In the above example, after you bluff the pot has $80 in it and your opponent must only call $10 to try to win the pot. He is getting 8-1, and he has already announced that his hand was good by betting in the first place, so he is highly likely to call.

Most of the times your opponent doesn't call the raise will be the ones where he was bluffing the river. And if your opponent was bluffing that means that your hand, which is a bluff as well, might have some chance of being a better hand anyway. So you should mainly reserve raise bluffs for times when you think there is a good chance that your opponent is bluffing and your hand is so bad that it probably can't even beat a bluff. If you have anything at all, like maybe a small pair or ace high, you are probably better off just taking the 6-1 pot odds and calling. But if you were drawing at a 6 high flush and missed and know your hand can't possibly win, then a raise bluff might be in order if you think your opponent might have been drawing at a flush too. As you can see, it is a very advanced play and therefore not one I recommend making very often.

Bluffing with Cards Left to Come

So far the only bluffs I have been talking about are river bluffs. Of course bluffing can and does occur on the flop and turn as well, and if you are planning to only bet that one street and then give up if your bluff fails the mathematics are the same. But if you are going to have to make more than one bet you are going to have to factor that into the equation.

Let's say that we are on the turn with one opponent in a $5/$10 game and the pot contains the same $60. You are considering betting the turn, which you are positive your opponent will call, and then the river with a hand that is most certainly not the best and not going to improve. This changes your odds quite a bit. Now losing costs us $20, but winning nets us $70 (the $60 in the pot plus the $10 your opponent calls on the turn). So the odds we are getting are

7-2, meaning that your bluff must succeed two out of nine times, or roughly 22 percent of the time, to be correct.

Notice that these odds, which are 4.5-1, are worse than the 6-1 odds we were getting in the above example. So it is easy to see mathematically that we should try bluffs like this less often. Furthermore, finding situations where this is a realistic consideration is much harder to begin with. This is a fancy play and something you should only try a very small percentage of the time. If they do and you think it is worth it, go ahead and give it a try, but for the most part I would avoid it. Besides, in the next chapter I am going to give you a much better way to bluff with cards left to come.

Selling a Bluff

So far we have seen that we should only bluff a small amount of the time, mainly because most opponents will call a large amount of the time. So when should we bluff? The idea is to do it when it is most likely to succeed. If you are going to bluff one in seven times, it might as well be the one chance in seven that appears most likely to work. The way to do that is to sell your bluff.

Selling your bluff means making it in a spot where your opponent can realistically put you on a good hand. The better an opponent thinks your odds are of having a good hand, the better the chances he will fold. So if you find yourself on the river and you think that it looks to your opponent as if you have a hand then you should be a lot more inclined to bluff then if your previous actions haven't given your opponent any reason to suspect he is beat.

This is often one of the biggest mistakes I see rookie players make. They play a hand very weak the whole way and then, at the very end, decide to just bet out when a brick comes. They are going to get called nearly every time because their opponent can't put them on a good hand.

Here is an example of selling a bluff. Suppose you hold a hand like:

and the flop comes:

Your opponent bets the flop and you raise for a free card. The turn is a brick making the board look like:

Your opponent checks and you check behind him. Now he realizes that you raised the flop for a free card. Let's suppose the river puts a heart on board making it look like:

If your opponent checks here you might want to try to bet. You have good reason to believe that he suspects you of a draw, and a flush draw would be a very obvious hand for him to put you on. He might be inclined to fold something here that has you beat.

Conclusion

So we see that bluffing, like much of poker, can be explained mathematically. It's fairly easy to see just how frequently a bluff needs to succeed for it to be a good bet. That is where the second element of poker, psychology, comes into play. A greater understanding of your opponents will enable you to determine their calling frequency with much greater accuracy and enable you to exploit them if they call too much or too little.

The same is also true in defending against bluffs. If we can get into an opponent's head and know how often he or she is inclined to bluff, then we can easily determine just how often to call them. And if they bluff too frequently or too infrequently we can exploit that as well by adjusting our calling standards.

By thinking about what hand your opponent puts you on you can determine just how likely a bluff is to succeed. Opponents generally are more likely to fold when they can put you on a hand and less likely when they can't.

Semi-Bluffing

He fakes a bluff.
—Ron Fairly

Up until now most of the bluffing I have been talking about has been pure bluffing where you have no hand and no draw. But there is a much more powerful form of bluffing available when there are cards still left to come known as semi-bluffing. Semi-bluffing means betting when you don't have the best hand but have a good draw at becoming the best hand.

The advantage to this is fairly easy to see. Semi-bluffing is much more powerful than bluffing because you have two ways to win. If you run a pure bluff your only chance to win the pot is to get your opponents to fold. With a semi-bluff you can win if they fold or if your hand improves. Let's look at an example.

Suppose you have:

and the board looks like:

Now you don't figure to have a better hand than your opponent but if you bet you can win either if your opponent folds or if your opponent calls and the river is a 4 or a 9, giving you a straight. So even if your opponent calls you there is still an 8 out of 46 chance that you will win.

For a semi-bluff to be a good bet the combination of the two ways of winning must add up to a positive EV. Therefore it is easy to see that the more likely it is that you will win the pot immediately the less likely your hand must be to improve if called for the bluff to remain good. So a hand that has few outs should only semi-bluff when it has a higher chance of stealing the pot. The opposite is true as well, meaning that a hand that has a high chance of improving to the best hand needs less chance of stealing immediately for the semi-bluff to remain profitable.

Still for a hand to be a semi-bluff it does need those two ways to win. Against opponents who will call down with anything semi-bluffing is not a good idea. You now can only win by making your hand. If betting or raising your draw has a positive EV anyway then by all means do so, but most of the time it will likely be better to try to draw as cheaply as possible.

How to Semi-Bluff

Semi-bluffing, like regular bluffing, can also be accomplished by raising or even check-raising. Still it is important to keep in mind that your implied odds on such maneuvers will generally be worse than when betting. And your odds of success will generally be poorer as well. Nonetheless occasions do present themselves to astute players and should one arise, be sure to take it.

The most common semi-bluffs are with flush draws or straight draws. Straight draws are probably the better of the two since your hand will often be disguised if it comes. People are much more suspicious of a semi-bluff with a flush draw on board because it is easy to spot, and for the same reason they may be less likely to pay you off if you hit.

Still, semi-bluffs are not limited to just those two draws. Something like bottom pair and a gutshot might be a good hand to semi-bluff with since you will often figure to have at least six outs. Two over-cards and a gutshot might be a great hand as well since you could have as many as ten outs. And if you felt your bluff had a good chance of succeeding immediately even hands with only a few outs would still qualify as a semi-bluff, tough perhaps just barely.

Buffs and Semi-Bluffs as Deception

The semi-bluff, like the regular bluff, also adds a lot of deception to your play. An opponent who only bets when he has a good hand is very easy for an observant player to play against. An opponent who could be betting a made hand, a drawing hand, or nothing at all is a much harder player to read. Thus bluffing and semi-bluffing are an essential part of a well-rounded game.

A lot of players talk about the advertising value they get from buffing. This means the deception value they get from getting caught. Once a player gets caught bluffing once or twice his opponents are going to have to be much more careful in the future about folding to him. They are going to have a harder time reading him and will pay him off more when he has the best hand.

Advertising value should be viewed as a good side effect of a bluff and not a reason to make one. The only time it should sway you toward bluffing would be if the bluff was basically an even money proposition anyway. Then the bluff would actually have a positive value due to the advertising effect. That effect is so small that you should not be making bluffs that are even mildly unprofitable just for the advertising.

When Opponents Semi-Bluff

The semi-bluff is such a powerful weapon that it is often hard to defend against when an opponent uses it. In fact in many cases where you suspect that there is a good chance that your opponent is semi-bluffing, you should actually consider folding. Suppose you see a flop heads up in a $10/$20 game for only one bet, putting $20 in the pot. Your opponent bets with a hand and you think there is a 40 percent chance that he has you beat (and if he does you are drawing dead) and a 60 percent chance that he merely has a flush draw. If he has a flush draw though he has about a

1/3 chance of beating you anyway by catching it on the turn or river. So he will win the 40 percent of the time that his hand is best and 1/3 of the 60 percent of the time that his hand isn't the best (20 percent) so a total of 60 percent of the time. He is now a favorite over you. If you knew that you were going to have to call him on every street (this investing $50) so your EV for doing so would be:

EV = (0.4 * $70) – (0.6 * $50)
EV = $28 – $30
EV = -$2

Note that when you win you profit $70 (the $20 preflop plus the $50 your opponent bet on the last three rounds). When you lose you only lose the $50 you called on the last three rounds. Still we see that even though your hand is the best 60 percent of the time on the flop you should just go ahead and fold it. In small pots you should be more inclined to just allow your opponent to win the pot immediately, even if you think it is more likely than not he is semi-bluffing. Of course the more likely you thought it was that he was semi-bluffing the less pot odds you would need to fold.

Similarly an opponent would be making a mistake by calling you in the same spot, even if he thought there was a 60 percent chance that you were semi-bluffing. This is very counterintuitive as we naturally feel inclined to call an opponent we think is likely to be bluffing. Most players will automatically call any time they think an opponent is more likely than not to be bluffing. Use that to your advantage.

Deception

Whether he likes it or not, a man's character is stripped bare at the poker table; if the other players read him better than he does, he has only himself to blame. Unless he is both able and prepared to see himself as others do, flaws and all, he will be a loser in cards, as in life.

—Anthony Holden

Deception is one of the most important and most misunderstood concepts in all of poker. It is important because without deception, a good opponent would never make a mistake. And it is misunderstood because most people don't have any idea how to go about deceiving their opponents the correct way.

Watching players play limit poker these days I see so many people making the worst plays in order to deceive their opponents, plays which cost far more than the value gained from their deception. They routinely slowplay hands which would they would be much better off playing fast, often costing themselves pots or forcing them to put in a lot of bets later when someone sucks out on them. They make bad bluffs just for the advertising value. They are costing themselves more than the deception is worth. The problems stem from their lack of understanding of what deception really is and why it is valuable.

What Deception Does

The basic idea behind deception is to make it hard for your opponents to read you. When a player reads you what he is doing is putting you on a range of holdings. A range of holdings is a mental list that one player keeps of all of the hands an opponent could possibly have based on the way they have played. A player who reads opponents well is one who can consistently and accurately keep their opponents on a narrow range of holdings. The narrower a range a player can keep his opponents on, the better at reading he is and the better his decisions will be.

Let's suppose everyone knows you only raise aces or kings preflop. When you raise your opponents can put you on a very narrow range of holdings. It would be very hard to make a mistake against you since your opponents know right where you are. In order to widen the range of holdings that your opponents must put you on you would have to raise more hands. If you raise, say, any pair and any ace preflop your opponents now have to have 25 hands in their range of holdings for you when you raise preflop instead of two. This will lead to them making poorer decisions both preflop and on later betting rounds.

This concept applies to any betting round in poker. Suppose you are up against an opponent who always bets the flop when he hits top pair. If that opponent checks to you now you know that he doesn't have top pair and can play accordingly. You can eliminate from his range of possible holdings all hands that make top pair.

If, however, that same opponent sometimes bets top pair and sometimes check-raises it then you won't be able to tell whether or not he has top pair when he does check to you, so you can't narrow down his range of holdings by eliminating top pair hands. You would have to bet the flop and see if he check-raises to get any information. If you further know that he often bets or check-raises draws (and sometimes even nothing at all) now his actions on the flop are giving you very little information at all. You can't eliminate anything from his range of holdings when he bets or check-raises.

The Value of Deception

Deception has a numerical value attached to it. The wider a range of holdings an opponent must put you on, the less able he is to make the correct play and the higher the value of your deception. If you could consistently limit an opponent to one hand you would never make a mistake against him—you would always know the exact, most profitable play. If you had to always consider that he could have many different hands you would have a much tougher time pegging down the correct play and your EV would be drastically lower than if you knew his hand exactly.

It is easy to see though that deception has a limited value. Consider your preflop play. If you raised every single hand then your opponents would never be able to put you on anything. The range of holdings they put you on would have to contain every hand in the deck, so in their mind you could have anything from 3 high to pocket aces. It would be much

harder for them to make the correct play both preflop and on the flop than it would if they could put you on a small range of hands. Unfortunately though, if you raised every hand preflop you would be putting in so much money with poor holdings that all of the deception in the world couldn't possibly make you a winning player. So you must try to find a happy medium where the amount you are spending for your deception is less than the value of the deception.

Note that deception only has any value at all against opponents who are putting you on a range of hands. Opponents who do not do so, which are invariably bad players and are very common at the lowest limits, only think of their own hand. Against players like that deception has no value at all. They play every hand as if you could have every holding in the deck. Often you will see very passive players (who only raise when they have the nuts) raise and get called by guys with top pair. The guy who calls with top pair there isn't someone you want to waste any money trying to deceive. You don't need to bluff at him to get him to call your bets later with weak holdings, he will do it anyway.

Remember too that even though most people don't know what a range of holdings is they are intrinsically putting you on one. They might not be able to give it a name or even know it exists, but as long as they are even trying to read you at all it is there. So the principle applies to anyone who is trying to read their opponents, even if they don't know what reading their opponents really means.

Basic Forms of Deception

I talked a bit in the chapter on semi-bluffing about how that can be a very good form of deception. Semi-bluffing frequently forces your opponent to consider that you might have one of various drawing hands in addition to a good hand. It also is a play that can have an immediate expectation and can actually be the optimal play quite frequently. So there are many cases in which semi-bluffing is both an excellent play and an excellent means of deception. This is a win-win situation for you and is why you always see experts semi-bluffing frequently in limit Hold'em.

In the chapter on position I also talked about how check-raising is a form of deception. It helps alleviate some of the disadvantages of being out of position on a hand. An opponent who doesn't check-raise gives away far too much information when he does check. Be sure to incorporate a decent amount of check-raising into your game.

One very valuable and completely overlooked way to deceive your opponents (I have yet to see this in print anywhere) is to play more hands. Mike Caro once pointed out that two different players can play two different amounts of hands and make the same amount because so many hands are marginal, meaning that they are either break even or very close to it. Many poker books advise you to merely fold these hands but in doing so you are missing a great cost-free way to force your opponents to add more hands to their mental list of your possible holdings.

Let's suppose that under the gun 20 percent of hands are profitable and the next 10 percent are marginal. These numbers are entirely fictional and only meant to illustrate a point, so don't go running off to play 30 percent of your hands under the gun. Anyway let's assume that some of those marginal 10 percent are mildly profitable, some break even, and some mildly unprofitable and that you can't tell which are which. Let's further assume that you do know that the 10 percent of marginal hands add up to $0 in EV if you played them all preflop. My advice is to play all of those 10 percent as well as the profitable 20 percent.

To see why just put yourself in your opponents' shoes. If you have a guy who raises 20 percent of hands under the gun you have a much better idea what he is holding than if he raises 30 percent of hands. Now when you play against him you will be able to make better decisions, both before and after the flop, and your better decisions cause you to profit off of him. Against the player who played 30 percent of hands, your decisions, while still possibly quite good, will invariably be worse over the long run than they are against the guy who played 20 percent of hands because you have to widen your range of his possible holdings. So his playing that extra 10 percent of hands, even though their cumulative EV is $0, is going to make his other 20 percent of hands more profitable.

The only downside to playing those extra 10 percent is that it is going to add to your fluctuations. Even though they may be break even hands in the long run, in the short run they can add up to a good win or a hefty loss. This will increase your swings a little. I will talk a little bit more about fluctuations and bankroll management and how this should influence what limits you play in a bit.

Mixing up Your Play

Deception is situation specific. By situation I am referring to both the board and the action on prior rounds. You will notice that players have a tendency to do the same thing any time they are faced with the same situation. It is very important not to do this. For instance a lot of players will always slowplay three of a kind when a pair flops on the board. If they hold:

and the flop comes:

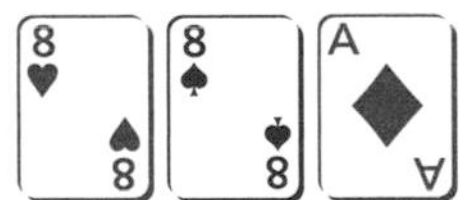

they will always check-call or call the flop and wait for the turn to check-raise or raise. Note that they are trying to do this to fool their opponents by waiting for later but since they do it every time they are actually telling an attentive observer (who notices that they slowplayed every they

flopped trips) exactly what they have. And when they do bet the flop that same observer will know that they don't have an eight and can play accordingly.

So to avoid giving away that sort of information you must mix up your play in each and every situation. In the above situation where you flopped trips there are actually two very good ways you could play. You could either lead out with a bet or check-raise. To be a deceptive player you should try to do a little of both. Exactly which one you choose should, for the most part, be the one that fits the situation better but not always. Sometimes you might want to lead out when a check-raise seems to be a slightly better play and vice versa.

The idea behind making plays that are suboptimal in order to deceive your opponents is to do it when the plays are only slightly suboptimal. In poker two plays often have very similar EVs, sometimes down to within a few cents. Times like that are perfect chances to mix up your play. There are many times where you flop trips and the decision between betting and check-raising is a very close call. In that case just try to pick one as randomly as possible and go with it.

Now it is very hard to remember each and every situation. It is probably even impossible to do so consciously. But it is certainly possible to get a feel for a number of very common situations such as the one above. What you must do, in order to train yourself to play deceptively, is to get a feel for how often you are taking each action. Are you only check-raising when you flop two pair or better? Maybe it is time to check-raise with a draw or a top pair a few times. Are you betting every draw? Maybe it is time to slow down and just check-call a few. Are you value betting every river? Maybe it is time to bluff induce a few.

While this seems like one very tough balancing act (and it is) keep in mind that subconsciously you remember everything that has ever happened in your life, everything that you have ever even seen. That is why it is so important to trust your instincts. You often hear expert players say that they just do what their instincts tell them. That is true because their instincts have been trained though years of study and experience and careful observation of the table they are sitting at. Their brain is subconsciously taking note of every situation and when a similar one comes up it might tell you, "Hey, buddy, you check-raised the last three times you flopped a set. Maybe you should bet this one out." Be sure to listen.

TEN

Slowplaying

If one is able and strong, then one should disguise oneself in order to appear inept and weak.

—Sun Tzu

Slowplaying in poker, often also referred to as trapping, means playing a hand softly on one street in order to entice an opponent into putting in a lot of money with an underdog on a later street where the bets are bigger. An example of this might be when you hold a hand like:

and the flop comes:

In this case you might want to simply check and call any bets and hope that the turn gives somebody something they might bet with. You pretty much flopped the entire board here.

Slowplaying is perhaps the most overused trick in the book. There are very few times when it is correct to slowplay. It should only even be considered in limit Hold'em when all of the following conditions are met:

1. It must be on a smaller betting round. In limit Hold'em this means the flop. In this case you are forsaking a small bet or two in favor of one or more large ones.

2. The pot must be small. If the pot is large it is more important to protect your hand than it is to try to squeeze out a couple extra bets. In a big pot opponents are also going to be much more likely to call or raise you with poor hands anyway.

3. Your hand must be very strong. The cards you are trying to give your opponent must have very little chance of making them a better hand or even a profitable draw to a better hand. If they did you would rather win the pot immediately than risk losing it to win an extra bet or two. Thus the minimum hand you should generally even consider slowplaying is a full house.

4. The free card you are giving must have a good chance of giving a good second best hand to someone who is likely to fold if you bet. If you flop a full house but there is a flush on board you would probably rather just bet out since anyone with a flush draw is likely to call you anyway. But if you flop quads on a rainbow board (like the above example) and the preflop betting suggests that nobody has a big pair you might want to let someone catch a flush draw, straight draw, or a top pair with a hand they might fold.

5. None of your opponents must appear to have a strong second best hand. If in the above example where you flopped

four eights you thought that one of your opponents had a big pair due to preflop betting you would probably still want to play your hand fast. They probably aren't going to fold it on the flop no matter what you do, so if the turn is one of the 2 cards that gives them a full house (for instance if they have pocket aces and an ace comes) you are going to make more by simply capping the flop, turn, and river. If the turn is a brick and you get aggressive after playing soft on the flop they might slow down and suspect that they are beat. In that case you probably will make one extra bet on the turn but sacrifice at least two small bets on the flop in the process, meaning that you won't make any more than you would have if you just got aggressive on the flop.

As you can see slowplaying is not correct very often. If you are ever in doubt as to whether or not you should slowplay I recommend not doing so. It is much better to err on the side of caution.

Please note that slowplaying is not the same as check-raising or bluff inducing. When check-raising you are playing a hand softly with the intent of raising later on the current betting round. And with bluff inducing you are playing a hand softly with the intent of squeezing an extra bet or two out of a hand that would likely fold, or saving bets against a better hand. Both of those plays are correct much more often than slowplaying.

Psychology

In some poker games in England, they have a rule that you're not allowed to talk about your hand during play. That's sick. Poker is a game based on the concept of talking your opponents into and out of pots. As I've said many times, there's nothing wrong with a wagering game involving pairs, straights, flushes, and full houses that is played in silence. Just don't call it 'poker.' That name is already taken.

—Mike Caro

Poker is a game of both math and psychology. We have already covered much of the mathematics involved in previous chapters. We have seen how simple equations can determine whether a play is correct if you have all of the necessary information. Unfortunately poker, unlike games like backgammon or chess, is a game of incomplete information. In chess you can see all of your opponent's pieces; in Hold'em, each of your opponents holds two cards which are unknown to you.

Range of Holdings

The good news is that using a little bit of psychology can help reveal your opponents' hands, or at least narrow down their range of holdings. As I said earlier an opponent's range of holdings is simply a list of each of the hands that they

could possibly have. For instance let's say through observation you notice that an opponent only raises pocket aces, pocket kings, pocket queens, and ace-king under the gun. If he raises under the gun then you can put him on that range of four hands. You can't possibly know which one of them he has, but just knowing his range of hands is very helpful.

Using mathematics you can determine how likely he is to have each hand. There are six ways to make pocket aces. You could have A♥ A♠, A♥ A♦, A♥ A♣, A♠ A♣, A♣ A♦, or A♣ A♦. There are also six ways to make kings and six ways to make queens. There are sixteen unique ways to make ace king making a total of thirty-four unique hands your opponent can have. He is equally likely to have each of them, which means that six out of thirty-four times he has aces, six out of thirty-four times he has kings, six out of thirty-four times he has queens, and sixteen out of thirty-four times he has ace king (four of which are suited).

Now we can use that information against our opponent. Of course in this case we would simply fold just about everything, since almost no hand could be worth playing. If we had an ace, king, or queen in our hand we would have to adjust the range above and subtract all of the hands featuring the card we hold. So if we held, say, Q♣ Q♠ we then know that there is only one way our opponent can have queens (Q♥ Q♦) so the odds of him having AK are now sixteen out of twenty-nine. Still here we would probably just fold, since out of twenty-nine times our opponent has us tied once, beaten twelve times, and is only a slight underdog (QQ beats AK about 55 percent of the time) the other sixteen times. Using computer simulations it turns out that our queens will only win 40 percent of the time if our opponent has that particular range of holdings. (See my website for information on free software to run your own such simulations.) And when you consider post-flop play you see that a lot of the times we lose to aces or kings we will lose a lot of money.

Now let's say an opponent raises and you think he would do that with any pair down to tens and any two cards ten or better. Suppose you have the aforementioned Q♣ Q♠. If you run a computer simulation using that range of holdings it turns out you are about a 68 percent favorite. Furthermore, flop play favors you, as a lot of times your opponent might hit a good second best hand, whereas many of the times you lose an overcard will flop and save you some money. So in this case you would want to re-raise and dump the money in while you are ahead.

Of course you can't do these computer simulations at the table, but you can do them at home when you are reviewing sessions later. And after doing a number of them you will find situations come up that you have already run through the simulations, and you will know your rough odds of winning. That is why it is so important to review your play after you are done. Similar situations pop up all the time, and learning from past hands will help you in the future.

When you hear people mention reading hands, this is what they are talking about. The better you read your opponents the smaller a range of holdings you can put them on. If you can consistently and accurately put your opponents on a tight range of holdings you stand to make much more than a player who can't do so. You will often be able to make laydowns that someone who can't read hands as well won't be able to and you will save money. You will also be able to call with some hands that opponents might fold and stop pots from being stolen from you. And you might even find a few more opportunities to make a good bluff.

Observation

If the above all seems a bit complicated, don't worry. You don't have to be that technical to win at poker. It sure doesn't hurt, but before we worry too much about how to employ such information we should learn how to gather it. The way we gather information is through observation.

Often when you are at a table, if you look around you will see that people who aren't involved in the hand are not watching what is going on. They are watching a television somewhere, talking—doing anything but watching the hand that is being played. These people are passing up on a lot of profit; don't be one of them.

By watching hands as they are played you can gain a lot of information on your opponents. By seeing how many hands they play and how they play them, you can gauge how loose or tight they are, how passive or aggressive. Do they bluff a lot? If so, you know to call them. Do they fold anytime a flush comes and someone bets? If so, then use that against them.

Most of your information gathering will be subconscious anyway, and that is fine. You don't need to count and see exactly what percentage of hands each person plays in each position. Just watch them and see what they roll over at the end of a hand, and you will get a feel. Even just one hand can tell you a lot about someone. For instance, suppose you see someone call a raise with a hand like Q♠ J♦. Now we know that means they overvalue big cards, and it is pretty safe to say that they would also call a raise with anything better than queen jack. If you see someone limping under the gun with 3♥ 4♥ you know that they are highly prone to playing suited connectors, even in bad position, and that they would certainly also limp there with higher ones such as 8♠ 9♠. And if they limp with it in early position you know they are definitely limping with all of that junk in middle or late position and probably adding a bunch of suited one-gaps (like 7♦ 9♦) as well. Just seeing that one limp with 43s allows you to add large numbers of hands to their ranges.

Levels of Thinking

In poker, players can think on a few different levels. Generally the more advanced a player is the higher a level he is thinking on. You should be thinking on at least three levels whenever you play. The levels are:

1. What do you have? This is the simplest level; you merely look at your hand and the board and figure out how strong it is.

2. What does your opponent have? This is a bit more complicated as you have to try to pin him down to as narrow a range of holdings as you can.

3. What does your opponent think that you have? This is even more complicated as you have to evaluate your own play from the standpoint of a player who hasn't seen your hole cards, which can be hard to do since you have seen your hole cards. Your table image (more on that later) and the way you have played so far in the current hand factor in highly here.

4. What does your opponent think that you think that he has? Here you are trying to figure out his level 3 thought process. Of course if your opponent doesn't think that deep it will be less important but still not unimportant, because though he may not pay that much mind consciously he is definitely doing so subconsciously. His subconscious thought may manifest itself in his play so it can still be helpful to be aware of it even though you would give it less weight than you would against a player who can think on that level consciously.

As you can imagine, the levels could theoretically go on forever but anything much beyond level four is too complicated to worry about. Trust me when I say that you can go pretty far up the poker chain and not run into many people who even think clearly on that level, let alone above it.

Nonetheless it is hard to win at any significant stakes without incorporating the first three levels into your thought process since so many players will be thinking, either consciously or subconsciously, on level 3. Like everything else in life your ability to think on these higher levels will grow as you gain experience. You should be able to think on at least level 2 right from the beginning and level 3 after a little experience. Beyond that things start to get a bit murky, and it may take you some time to get to level 4. Don't worry though, there is plenty of money to be made before you can truly think like that.

Table Image

Your table image is basically the way opponents at the table perceive you. Do they perceive you as being loose or tight, passive or aggressive? It is important to know. How they perceive you affects how they play hands against you, and if you know both what your table image is and how they change their play according to it you can more easily read them.

Remember that table image can sometimes be inaccurate. If a player sits at your table and raises the first five hands and pounds them all the way you may think he is a maniac, especially if he didn't show them. It is, however, entirely possible that he just got five consecutive monster hands. He could in fact be a very weak tight player who just picked up big pairs five hands in a row, and if that is the

case chances are people will have a very inaccurate perception of him.

Determining what people think of you is often hard. It has a lot to do with how you have played recently. Many people don't pay attention to hands they aren't involved in, so their perception of you will be dominated more by hands in which you and they were both involved. If there were a lot of hands like that they may think you a loose player; if not, they may think you a tight player. If you were raising a lot in those hands they will likely think you an aggressive player; if not, they may think you passive.

Players who pay more attention will have a much better idea of how you really play. Even they will tend to heavily weight your recent play, which is not necessarily a bad idea either. As the night drags on tight players who are having bad luck often turn into loose ones and vice versa. People's emotional states often change and their play follows. So be aware of how you have been playing recently.

That being said, many people form one image of you and are to reluctant to change it. Don't fall into this trap. As I said earlier if a player comes in and is aggressive with his first five hands he may seem to be a maniac. Chances are he is, but if he proceeds to fold every hand for the next hour be sure to update your opinion of him.

Also, be very aware that how a player plays preflop and post-flop are very different. Some people play very tight preflop but then never seem to fold once the flop comes. Some people are the opposite, raising every hand before the flop and then playing very well after. Those players can be deadly. Be sure to think in terms of how each player plays on each street, not just how they play preflop.

Your table image is also greatly impacted by your appearances. They say you can't judge a book by its cover, but that doesn't stop most people from trying. If you are a young white male, people are going to be much more likely to peg you as an aggressive player. A young white female whose game is identical to that young white male's might be considered a calling station or weak-tight (playing few hands and doing so meekly). People's preconceptions often dominate their image of other players. Be aware of them and use them to your advantage.

I personally am a young white male with a shaved head. I am usually well dressed but not ostentatiously so. I wear a nice Movado watch, not cheap but not a Rolex either. People who see me sit down expect me to play aggressively. I am not sure why, maybe because most people who look like me are that way. In any case, by playing a moderately aggressive game I usually have everyone thinking I am another Gus Hansen wannabe. I am quite able to use this to my advantage. It scores me tons of extra bets. It does probably mean I have to be a bit more selective with my bluffs, but the extra action more than makes up for it in the end.

People see what they want to see; I suggest helping them out a little bit and using their perceptions to your advantage.

If you are an old white man and they see a rock before you even sit down at the table, then play tight but use that image to bluff a bit more to pick up a few extra pots. If you are a young Asian man wearing lots of gold and they see a maniac sitting down, then play moderately aggressively and capitalize on all of your good hands.

As far as judging opponents goes, don't put too much stock in stereotypes. People of all ages and ethnicities can be excellent players. You will run into some loose-aggressive old ladies and loose-weak young men; be sure to pay attention to how they play rather than to how they look.

SECTION II

Limit Hold'em Concepts

Preflop Play Introduction

Aces are larger than life and greater than mountains.
—Mike Caro

The first street in Texas Hold'em, which we will refer to here as preflop, is perhaps the most important street in the game. It is the foundation of a winning approach. Even a world class player couldn't win at a $3/$6 game if his preflop strategy was terrible. At the lowest limits, solid preflop play combined with even mediocre post-flop play might make you a winner.

Preflop play is also the easiest to teach, due to the relatively low amount of scenarios that can occur there. There are only 169 different starting hands, and many hands have a very similar EV, so we can even narrow them down into fewer than a dozen groups. Note that when counting the number of possible hands we assume that A♥ K♥ is the same as A♠ K♠ because both have equal chances of winning. This means that there are 13 pair hands (22-AA), and 78 different non-pair hands (we assume A♥ 4♠ is the same as A♥ 4♠ because both have exactly the same expectation) each of which can be either suited or unsuited. A♥ K♥ has a better chance of winning a pot than A♥ K♠ does (more on that in a minute) so we must count them as different hands, making 156 different non-pair hands and 13 pairs, for a total of 169 different hands.

This simplicity works for and against us. It does make it easier to teach proper preflop play, but it also makes it easier for your opponents to learn proper preflop play. As you rise through the ranks of the poker world, you will eventually hit a level where nearly everyone plays reasonably well at preflop. At that point, solid preflop play alone will not keep your head above water. But at lower limits, just playing well before the flop will keep you from being at a tremendous disadvantage while you learn to perfect your postflop play, which in the higher limits will be the most important part of your game.

Tight Play

In Hold'em it turns out that a relatively low percentage of starting hands are actually profitable. Most starting hands have a negative EV. In fact a good preflop strategy will have you folding more than three out of four of your hands right off the bat. This is called tight play and it is the best way to go about winning at limit Hold'em.

Many of today's players don't know that they should play tight or simply don't have the patience to. They play one unprofitable hand after another, either because they don't know any better or because they simply have more fun that way. They call with junky suited cards hoping to make a flush, or call raises with medium sized cards that are likely

to flop middle pair or be outkicked even if they do flop top pair. And if you are at a loose table all of that extra money in the pot does mean that you should play a little looser than you normally might, but you should still be one of the tightest people at the table. Simply by exercising a little patience and waiting for profitable hands you can beat the majority of the poker games spread today.

Basic Concepts

To understand preflop play you must first understand the concept that big cards are better than small ones. A hand like A♥ K♠ is a much better hand than one like 8♦ 7♣. This is pretty easy to understand because if both hands pair one of their cards the A♥ K♠ will win. If they both miss the board entirely the A♥ K♠ wins as well. Also if the 8♦ 7♣ pairs on the flop the A♥ K♠ has 6 outs (three aces and three kings) left in the deck to hit, but if the A♥ K♠ hits the flop then the 8♦ 7♣ must now make two pair to win.

Also you must understand that suited cards are better than unsuited cards of the same rank. This is because A♥ K♥ will hit the exact same amount of pairs, two pairs, and straights as A♥ K♠ but will hit many more flushes, and flushes (especially ace high) are strong hands in Hold'em. The odds of hitting a flush using only three cards from the board are many times greater than the odds of hitting it using four, so even though the unsuited A♥ K♠ can make two flushes it is still much less likely to do so than its suited cousin. Also note that the suited one will always have the best possible flush, whereas if four spades come, the unsuited A♥ K♠ above would lose to any hand with the ace of spades.

To determine which hands to play, you have to consider how your opponents' preflop and postflop play is going to effect them. So we are going to examine the four main types of hands: pocket pairs, big card hands, drawing hands, and rag hands. Then I will try to explain in which instances each type of hand becomes optimal and what sort of action it prefers.

Pocket Pairs

The first type of hand is the pocket pair. As far as pocket pairs go, bigger is obviously better. It is very easy to see why Q♠ Q♥ is a better hand than 4♠ 4♥ because there are so many pairs your opponent can have that beat 4s but not queens. In most cases though the difference between two adjacent pairs (say 4s and 5s) is pretty small. It still exists, but there is only one pair which is very much better than the next pair below it, and that is pocket aces. Pocket aces are by far the best hand in Texas Hold'em and are much more profitable than kings, mostly duc to postflop considerations.

The pocket pair has two main ways to win. It can either be the best hand (if nobody hits a bigger pair) or it can hit three of a kind (known as a set). Obviously the bigger the pair is the more likely it is to win without hitting a set. While pocket aces will usually stand up with no improvement even against multiple opponents, pocket deuces will almost always need to hit three of a kind in order to beat a few other hands.

A set is a very strong hand in Hold'em as it will often be

the best hand, and even when it isn't, it has very good odds of turning into a full house.

Big Card Hands

Big card hands (like A♣ K♠) are hands whose primary value lies in hitting something like top pair. If you hit a pair with A♣ K♠ then you have a very good chance of winning the pot. Your opponents need to get two pair or better to beat you, because you have the best pair and the best kicker. Opponents do hit two pair or better sometimes, but you will probably win more often than not when you hit a flop with AK.

Also note that AK is a much better hand than AQ. With AQ you can flop an ace and still lose to AK. Or you can flop a queen but a king can hit and give someone else top pair. The difference between AK and AQ is huge, just like the difference between pocket aces and pocket kings. Unlike with pairs though, each notch down the big card ladder is significantly lower than the previous, so a hand like AQ is sometimes not even playable, whereas you would almost never fold AK before the flop. And with a hand like AT, you might fold more often than not in certain positions.

Drawing Hands

Hands which we will call drawing hands (things like suited connectors, suited aces, or straight cards like 10♦ 9♣) are those whose primary value lies in hitting something like a straight or a flush. Hands like 7♦ 6♦ don't have much chance of ending up with top pair, and even if they do you may lose for having too small of a kicker or being up against an overpair. If you play a hand like that you are really hoping to flop a straight or a flush or at least a draw to one.

Some hands, like A♥ K♥, are both big cards and drawing hands, and they have two ways to win. These hands are very valuable. The whole, in this case, is greater than the sum of its parts, so a hand like this should be treated as a premium holding. Even hands like A♥ Q♥ or K♠ Q♠ are very strong. In fact a lower ranked unsuited hand is often more valuable than a higher ranked suited hand (especially in loose games), so often A♣ 10♣ is a better hand than A♠ J♥. The further you go down the big card scale the more valuable being suited becomes, so a hand like A♦ 2♦ is often much more valuable than even A♣ 7♥, even though the second card is five ranks lower.

Rag Hands

These are the hands that you are going to avoid ever putting any bets in with preflop, junk like 10♣ 5♥. These hands can't make any good flushes or straights and they don't have much chance of winning with top pair. They can hit two pair or three of a kind, but even then they easily beaten by a higher two pair or trips. You will see some flops with hands like this out of the big blind (and maybe the small blind in certain games) but probably shouldn't be voluntarily investing any money on this garbage.

Table Conditions

The value of each of the above types of hands fluctuates depending on table conditions. Each of those types of hands (except rags, which are always unprofitable and will be ignored here) prefers a certain type of action. Let's look at each of the main types of hands and see when they are optimal.

Optimal Game Conditions for Pocket Pairs

It is important to differentiate the pocket pairs according to size, so we will call them small, medium, big, and aces, which is in a category of its own. Let's examine small pairs first.

Small pairs (like 2 2 or 6 6) have little chance of winning without hitting a set, but when they hit a set they become very strong hands. So ideally you would like to be able to put in as little money as possible preflop. Then if you miss your set (which you will about seven out of eight times), you can fold easily. On the other hand, if you hit your set, you would then like to be able to put a lot of money in the pot, as your hand is now very strong and can beat numerous opponents. So for small pairs the ideal game conditions would be one where a lot of people are playing preflop (loose) and there is not much raising (passive). After the flop you would ideally want loose action still but now you want there to be a lot of raising (aggressive), so our ideal game for small pocket pairs would be one that is loose-passive preflop and loose-aggressive postflop.

By that theory then the worst games for pocket pairs would be ones which are tight-aggressive preflop and then tight-passive postflop. Most games are generally the same preflop as they are postflop, so neither of the above conditions are very common, especially at lower limits. You are mainly going to be faced with games that are loose-passive or tight-aggressive the whole way through, so just try to focus more on the preflop table conditions than the postflop ones.

Large pocket pairs (we will loosely define these here as JJ and up) have a considerable chance of winning without improving. The fewer opponents they are up against the greater the chance they have of winning, so they prefer a game where there are few opponents seeing the flop. In a tight-aggressive game these hands can reraise to isolate opponents (who may very well even be dominated) and win unimproved, so these are the games that they most prefer. With a big pair hand you want to raise and eliminate opponents if it is likely to get the pot short handed.

However, in games where a lot of people are seeing the flop, you should still play big pairs, as they are still very profitable. A hand like JJ or QQ isn't very likely to win against six or seven opponents without improving, but like small pairs, it is worth trying to hit a set. And it will sometimes win, even against a full nine opponents, without improvement as well. So if you can't get the pot down to just a few people then you still want to play the hand, be sure not to dump in a lot of money when someone starts reraising.

Pocket aces (and to a lesser extent kings) are a very unique hand in that what happens preflop doesn't really matter. Your hand has a good chance of holding up no

matter how many people enter the pot. More people entering the pot means more chance of you losing, but it also means more money when you win. So when you get a hand like that all you want to do is stuff the money in the pot. Raise and reraise as much as you can. If you only get one or two opponents that's fine. If you get nine opponents, that's fine too. And if you get four or five, great. Aces are always the best hand preflop, and kings are the best hand the vast majority of times, too. Both are often very hard to lay down when someone beats them after the flop (the exception is when you have KK and an ace flops, in which case folding can become easier) so you might as well jam the pot while you know you are a huge favorite.

Medium pocket pairs, which we will define here as 77-TT, have considerably more chance of winning unimproved than small ones, especially if they can get the pot down to just one or two opponents, but their chances still aren't all that good. These hands actually prefer either games just like those that favor the small pairs (lots of passive action preflop) or those that favor the big ones (few opponents seeing the flop). What they don't like are games in the middle, where four or so people are routinely seeing the flop for a few bets. In this case there are too many opponents for the hand to have much chance of winning unimproved, and too few opponents to make it worth trying to hit a set, especially if opponents are playing well after the flop. You probably will still play the majority of them no matter what the game conditions, but they will make you less profit.

Optimal Game Conditions for Big Cards

Big card hands (like AK) are best when played against a small number of people. The fewer opponents you have drawing to beat you the better. A good pair with a good kicker is strong against few opponents, but against many it is probably going to take something better to win. Big cards also like to get the small pairs and drawing hands to put in as much as possible before the flop to reduce their implied odds so in general you should be trying to narrow the field with hands like these when you play them. Of course if there are already a large amount of limpers and you can't get the pot down to just a couple of opponents, you might decide to just limp with a hand like K♥ J♣ and try to hit a good flop—but be careful with just one pair if you hit it.

Optimal Game Conditions for Drawing Hands

Drawing hands play best in loose-passive games. Consider a hand like 6♦ 7♦, where you really want to flop a flush or straight draw. Most times you are going to miss the flop and fold, so ideally you would want to get in cheaply on the first betting round. When you do flop a draw, you will have a higher EV if you can continue on cheaply with a lot of opponents who will pay you off if you make your hand, so an all-around loose-passive game is best.

Optimal Game Conditions for Big Suited Cards

Big cards play well against few opponents, and drawing cards play well against many. So it should come as no surprise that hands that are both big card hands and drawing hands,

like K♣ Q♣, play well no matter how many opponents they are up against. Furthermore you can choose to either to narrow the field with them (play them like big cards) or let a lot of limpers in (play them like drawing hands) depending on game conditions.

Game Condition Summary

Exactly which hands you should see the flop with in Hold'em depends on a few things. In the next chapter I will give specific preflop recommendations, but for now let's review how table conditions should affect your preflop play. If your table is loose then you should be playing looser as well (though not as loose as everyone else) because now there is more money in most pots, making more hands profitable. If your table is tight then you should be playing tighter because the small pots lower your EV. Post-flop this reverses a bit, as you then will want to tighten up more at loose tables and play more hands (aggressively) at tight ones, but we will deal with that later.

For now suffice it to say that before the flop the looser your opponents play, the looser you should play, and the tighter they play, the tighter you should play. So in essence the amount of hands you play is determined by the amount of hands your opponents play.

Your opponents' aggression level is also important—it influences which cards you play. If your opponents are very aggressive before and after the flop, then you want to play big cards and pairs. This is because if you flop a good hand (top pair with a good kicker if you hold big cards, or three of a kind or an over-pair if you hold a pocket pair) you can play it aggressively and get your opponents to put in a lot of money with a dominated hand. You can also charge the drawing hands to draw at you, reducing their EV and therefore increasing yours.

In aggressive games drawing hands aren't as valuable because you are going to have to pay through the nose to try to hit a straight or a flush. We saw in the chapter on mathematical expectation how betting makes drawing hands less profitable. Also, aggressive opponents are much more likely to make you put in multiple bets preflop, which greatly reduces your implied odds on a hand like 7♦ 8♦ . So if your game is aggressive you should be less inclined to play drawing hands and more inclined to play big cards and pairs.

If your opponents are playing passively then drawing hands increase in value. Now you are likely to get to draw cheaply and get paid off by a few people when you hit, so you should be more inclined to play them. Big cards decrease in value because you are less likely to get your opponents to put in a lot of money with dominated hands. And you are going to be up against a lot of drawing hands, many of which are getting proper odds (at your expense) to continue on after the flop.

For the big pairs any game is a good game. A hand like aces, kings, or queens is going to be largely profitable in any game you find. Those hands have such an incredible chance of winning without hitting a set (especially if the

field can be narrowed to one or two opponents) that they are always going to be winners in the long run. So we are going to play big pairs pretty strong no matter what the game conditions are.

You will notice throughout your poker career that most loose players and games tend to also be passive, and most tighter players and games tend to be more aggressive. This is certainly not an absolute as you will run across loose-aggressive or tight-passive opponents and sometimes even games of that description, but it will be true more times than not.

So using the above recommendations we see that in loose-passive games we want to be playing more hands, and playing a lot of hands like suited connectors and pairs. A hand like 8♠ 9♠ will probably become more profitable than one like K♦ J♥ (though both may often be playable). In games where the opponents are tight-aggressive we are going to play fewer hands and lean more towards big cards than drawing hands.

THIRTEEN

Starting Hand Recommendations

As I stated earlier, position is of great importance in Texas Hold'em, and this is especially true before the flop. The ability to see what your opponents do before making decisions on later streets makes any hand more profitable in late position than it is in early position. Suppose you limp under the gun with 2♣ 2♦. You now have nine people behind you who can raise and re-raise. But if you are on the button, you already know what seven of your opponents have done preflop, so you can be much more confident that the pot won't get raised and re-raised behind you. Thus you can play more hands in late position than you can in early position.

In this chapter, I am going to talk about different positions; how you play in each of them is critical. The non-blind hands will be divided into three categories: early, middle, and late. The blinds will each occupy their own category. We will assume the game to be ten-handed, so that leaves eight non-blind positions. The first three we will call early position, the second three we will call middle, and the last two will be called late. If the game should become nine-handed, I recommend calling the first three early, then the next two middle and the last two late. For an eight-handed game, it

would be simply two, two, and two, and anything less will be covered in the short-handed section.

Furthermore games are often of one of two characters, either loose and passive or tight and aggressive. How many players you can expect to join a hand with you and how often you can expect them to raise has a great effect on what hands you should be playing, so I will give separate recommendations for the two games in both early and middle positions. In late position you already have a very good idea of how many players are going to be seeing the flop and how many bets it will cost to do so, so in late position I will only give recommendations based on what has happened already.

For the purposes of this book we will define a loose game to be one where an average of four or more players see the flop. A tight one would then be one where less than four players see the flop on average. I will assume that a loose game is passive and a tight game is aggressive. This is the case the majority of the time, and when it isn't simply use the basic preflop concepts outlined in the last chapter to adjust your play accordingly. For instance you know that hands like suited connectors love to see flops cheaply with a lot of people, so if your loose game also turns out to be very aggressive (making flops expensive) you are going to have to start throwing some of those away.

As you progress throughout your poker career you are going to have to start to think in less concrete terms. For instance the last seat of middle position should play a little different than the first. Using the basic concepts from the last chapter and some plain old experience will help you adapt. Nonetheless the following advice should lay a solid foundation for you to build your preflop standards around.

I am going to use a fairly standard poker literature convention here when giving starting hand recommendations. Rather than writing out that you should play aces, kings, queens, and jacks I will express that group as AA-JJ. I will use the same with both suited and unsuited non-pair hands to annotate a range of holdings with the same high card. So AKo, AQo, AJo, and ATo would be shown as AKo-ATo. If they were all suited it would be annotated as AKs-ATs. If I don't specify suited or offsuit then assume I mean both, so if I say to play AK-AT I mean play them whether or not they are suited. There isn't any reason why you would ever play an unsuited hand but not its suited brother anyway.

Early Position

In the first three seats after the big blind we are going to play some very tight poker, especially in tight games. In those seats you have no idea how many opponents are going to come in or how many bets it is going to cost to see the flop. Pretty much all you do know is that if you see a flop, you are likely to be at a positional disadvantage.

In loose games, you are still going to play fairly tight, but you can play a few more hands than you can in tight games. In a game where an early position limp is likely to get isolated a hand like JTs isn't very strong. In a loose pas-

sive game where most pots are multi-way for one bet, that hand can become very profitable.

Loose Games

First of all, there are the raising hands. In early position go ahead and raise AA-JJ and AK-AQ. You can also choose to limp with AKs or AQs as they do play well in multi-way pots, but raise them most of the time. Maybe choose one suit and always limp with that particular suit, which will have you raising 3/4ths of the time.

As far as calling hands, assuming the pot has not yet been raised, I recommend playing any two cards ten or better that are suited as well. I would also add KQ and AJ offsuit. Also any pair down to 8s is fine to limp with. If the game is extra loose you can go even further than that. I used to play in $3/$6 games where most flops were seven ways for one bet, and in games like that (which are rare). I recommend playing suited connectors down to 78s, suited one-gaps down to T8s, all suited aces, and pairs down to 5s. In a game in between (average of five or six players per flop), you would probably want to cut the suited connectors off at 98s and the pairs off at 7s or 6s. Suited one-gaps would go down to J9s. I wouldn't recommend playing suited aces below AT either.

If the pot has been raised ahead of you, it is time to play very tight poker. I would reraise with AA-QQ, AK, and AKs at any time. In fact those hands are an automatic raise no matter what happens, just bet away if you get them. I would call with JJ or TT and AQs. If the table is very loose and the raiser raises an above average amount of hands you might mix in 99, KQs, and AJs, but if you aren't sure you're probably better off folding.

Tight Games

Again AA-QQ, AK, and AKs are automatic capping hands so raise them no matter what. If there hasn't yet been a raise I recommend raising with JJ, TT, AQs, AQo, AJs, KQs as well. AJ off and 99 are a discretion call but if you feel that there is a good chance you are going to get three-bet and have to play out of position, then just go ahead and fold them. If the table is tight but somewhat passive and you feel there is a decent chance of a blind steal (especially if you are in the last early position seat) then go ahead and pop them and maybe 88 as well. KJ and KQ offsuit are folding hands as are any big cards lower than that regardless of suit.

As far as limping goes you shouldn't really be doing any of it if nobody has yet entered the pot. Once someone limps it changes the dynamic a bit because if you limp as well that makes two limpers and having two limpers tends to create a multi-way pot. Still I wouldn't be doing much limping. As the first person in the pot, I would raise all of the hands you would raise here except AJs and KQs which are OK to call with. Also limping with AQs rather than raising is an option, but I would lean heavily towards raising.

If the pot has been raised, now you must three-bet or fold. I would say that it would be okay to call with JJ or TT, but those would be about the only hands, and your observant

opponents would be getting too much information that way. They would eventually see that those were the only hands you call with there and know what you have whenever you do it. If the raiser has fairly loose standards then three-bet hands like JJ, TT, and AQs. If he has very tight standards then just go ahead and fold them. Any big cards AQ or below you should probably just fold unless the raiser is a maniac, in which case I would three-bet anything AJ or better and any pair 9s or better.

Middle Position

Middle position play is more complex than early position play. Now a few people have acted before us so we have a little bit more information. There are many more possible combinations of limpers and/or raisers ahead of us so the advice is going to have to take that into account.

With AA and KK I advise raising no matter what. With AK or QQ you would not raise only if it was three or four bets to you and you were certain that one of the raisers had to have AA or KK, in which case you would fold. Otherwise you want to raise with those hands as well.

Loose Games, No Limpers

If there are no limpers you should add to your raising standards. You can now safely raise AA-99 (8s and 7s as well in late middle) any AKs-ATs, AK-AJ, KQs-KJs, and KQ. If you are in early middle position you might go ahead and limp with KTs-JTs, QJs, and 88 or 77 if you still figure to get a couple callers behind you. If you are in late middle you might just pop them instead. Play them as big card hands at that point since so many people have folded ahead of you.

Loose Games, One Limper

Against one limper I recommend raising AA-TT, AKs-ATs, AK-AJ, and KQs. In late middle maybe add in 99 and KJs.

As far as limping goes I would treat it pretty much like you would early position. Limp with any two suited ten or better, suited connectors down to 9Ts, suited one-gaps down to T8s, and pairs down to 7s.

Loose Games, Two or More Limpers

Once two people have limped the feeding frenzy begins. Now raising isn't going to get the pot short-handed so I recommend only doing it with AA-QQ, AK, AKs. Limp with all of the hands you would against one limper but take pairs down to 5s and suited connectors down to 45s. Take one gaps down to 97s, and two gaps down to Q9s. Also limp with AQ-AJ, KQ-KJ, and QJ.

Loose Games, One or More Raises

If there is a raise and no callers, play the same way you would against a raise in early position. If there are callers then go ahead and call with JJ, TT, and AQs. That's about it; don't go calling with offsuit big cards or junk like suited connectors. And if there are two or more raises only queens or better or AK, and even those two hands aren't necessary if you are positive someone has KK or AA. That will be rare, but there are some times where you know a player would not

make it three bets cold without KK or AA, so if you have AK there just go ahead and fold.

Tight Games, No Limpers

If you are in middle position in a tight game and there are no limpers, you are now pretty much playing raise or fold. Limping is probably just going to get you isolated out of position and raising has a little more chance of stealing the blinds, so just go ahead and pop anything you decide to play. We are pretty much going to play big cards and medium and large pairs in this spot.

Here the hands I advise raising with are AA-88, AKo-AJo, AKs-ATs, KQo-KJo, and KQs-KJs. In late middle position you might throw in KTs, QJo, and QJs and a couple more pairs.

Tight Games, One Limper

If you are middle position and someone has limped then you should be more inclined to limp in yourself. That will make two limpers, which generally sets off a feeding frenzy, and you can expect to take a flop at least four-handed. You would, of course, raise any pair tens or better and any hand AQ or better. You would limp with all of the hands I recommend raising with in the above section plus suited connectors down to 87 and pairs down to 7s. You would also one to limp with suited one-gaps down to J9 or so and KTs.

Tight Games, Multiple Limpers

If you have two or more limpers in middle position you can now play a much wider range of hands. The more limpers, the more you can play. With three or more limpers I would come in with any pair, any suited connectors down to 45s, suited one-gaps down to 97s, suited two-gaps down to Q9, and any suited ace. Any two ten or above suited will work as well, so hands like KTs are fine. With only two limpers you might want to scale back the connectors and one-gaps a bit and maybe some of the small pairs and suited aces as well.

Tight Games, Raises

Treat this pretty much the same way you would in early position if there are no callers. If there are one or two you could add in a couple pairs (maybe down to 99) to call with, but for the most part play pretty tight when there is a raise.

Late Position

In late position, the texture of the game isn't as important anymore because you aren't trying to figure out what is going to happen. You already have a pretty good idea of how many players are going to see the flop and how many bets it is going to cost. The odds of something unexpected happening behind you are greatly reduced, so just play according to what has already transpired.

As far as calling raises, treat it like middle position, which pretty much means don't call many at all. You really

don't want to be calling a lot of raises in Hold'em; usually you would rather be raising yourself or folding.

Late Position, 0 or 1 Limpers

In late position if there are no limpers you are going to play raise or fold poker. Your aim is to steal the blind. Of course people know this so the blinds are going to call you a lot more than they would call an under-the-gun raiser, but you are still going to steal it immediately enough for raising to be better than calling. And most of the time you don't steal it you are going to get the pot heads-up. Remember that an opponent without a pair in the hole will only hit the board one-third of the time, so even if you get a call you can often just bet down the flop. Or you can just luck into a hand.

If there is one limper, then your goal is to isolate him or at least get the pot down to three people. If you get the pot heads-up or three-handed with you in position, you are in a profitable situation. So in late position with one limper, you are also playing raise or fold, and again be sure to try to bet down the pot on the flop.

In the situation where you have one caller you will probably want to raise any pair, any two 10 or better, and any suited ace. Suited connectors down to 87 and one gaps down to something like T8 are fine. Also a hand like K9s or Q9s would be okay to raise too. Remember, your hand has two ways to win here: you can hit the best hand or you can bet at some point (most likely the flop). You aren't really bluffing because you know the limper is going to call you, but you are helping to set up the bluff on the flop. You are going to be in position the whole way as well, so even if your hand is most likely not as good as your opponent's, your position and your high likelihood of betting the flop later may still make it profitable.

If there are no limper, you can raise a few more hands since you now have the ability to win the pot immediately. Any ace is fine here (suited or otherwise), as is any suited king. Suited two-gaps down to J8s are good and three-gaps down to K9s.

Late Position, 2 or More Limpers

In late position with multiple limpers you can play a lot of hands. The more limpers, the more hands you can play. Any pair, any suited ace, any suited connectors, suited one-gaps down to 75s, and two-gaps down to T7s. Any two 9 or better suited, any two 10 or better unsuited, all are fine limping hands. With only two or three limpers you'll definitely want to scale back some of the suited hands, but with four or more limpers play them all.

Now if there are a lot of limpers you may want to value raise some drawing hands—suited hands that play very well in multi-way pots, like JTs or AJs. You can even raise just to get more money in the pot. You could also apply this concept to pairs as well. Those hands all are looking to hit a big flop and are very easy to play. Since you have a lot of people in you might want to juice the pot for when they come in. This might also convince everyone to check to you if you miss so

you can take a free turn card and try to pick up the first half of a runner-runner draw or something.

You will of course want to value raise big hands like AA-TT and AKs. With big card hands other than AKs you will probably be better off just limping and trying to keep the pot small in case you do flop top pair. That way you can potentially raise and give all of the weaker drawing hands poor odds to call on the flop.

Blind Play

Play in the big blinds requires a few extra considerations. First of all you already have money in the pot, which makes calling or raising cheaper. Obviously if you are in the big blind and the pot has not yet been raised you can check and take a free flop, but a lot of hands are going to be raised, forcing you to make a decision. And in the small blind even if there has been no raise you have a decision to make.

When evaluating what to do you should consider a few things. First of all you have to consider that you are going to be out of position for the rest of the hand. Your relative position may actually be good if the first person in the pot raised though, so keep that in mind as well. Remember that the more people in the pot the less important position becomes but it always has some value.

You also you have to consider the increased odds you are getting. The money you have already put in the pot counts towards your calling, so if you post a $15 blind and it is raised once you only have to call $15 more whereas someone in middle position would have to call $30 cold. This greatly increases your implied odds as well, so you would be more inclined to call out of the blinds than you would to call in other positions.

If there is a raise, you have to consider where it came from. A raise under the gun generally means a much stronger hand than a raise from late position, especially if there were no limpers. A lot of people will raise the majority of their hands on the button or cutoff if it has been mucked around to them. You should be much more inclined to call a blind-stealing type raise than one from an earlier position, since you are far less likely to be dominated.

Small Blind Play

How you should play in the small blind depends greatly upon how big the small blind is. In a game where the small blind is 1/3 of the big blind (common in $3/$6) or 1/2 of the big blind (common in games like $10/$20 and $20/$40) you should treat it as if you were in late position if there are no raises.Your position is bad but your slightly increased odds and the fact that you probably aren't going to get raised make calling much easier. If there are any raises you should treat it the same way you would in middle position which pretty much means folding everything but premium hands.

The exception to this is when everyone has folded. In that case you should probably play it just like you were on the button and everyone had folded to you, raising any hand worth playing. You are going to be out of position the whole

way so if a hand is worth seeing a flop you might as well try to take it right there.

If the small blind is 2/3 of the big blind, then you should call with any two cards in a pot that hasn't been raised. Here your implied odds are far too great to fold any hand. If there has only been one limper you are getting 8-1 immediately, but your implied odds are fantastic because the bet on the flop is three times the size of the bet you must call. Following this advice will have you seeing some flops with seriously bad hands like J♥ 6♣. Be very careful not to get carried away with a hand like that if you flop top pair or something. When you put in that 1/3 bet you are hoping to flop at least two pair or preferably trips, but if you don't and there is any heat at all then get out of the kitchen quickly.

If the hand has been raised you are going to want to tighten up a bit. If there are a couple of limpers or cold callers then you will probably want to call most hands that you would call out of middle position with for no raise. If there aren't any limpers you are going to want to tighten up a bit, maybe throw away the poorer suited connectors and smaller pairs in that range.

Big Blind Play

In the big blind, which I am assuming to be equal to one small bet, you can call a raise a little more liberally than you can in the small blind because of your increased odds and implied odds. If there are a couple of limpers treat it just like you would treat late position with no raise. If there aren't then treat it like middle position; unless the raise appears to be a blind steal, then go back to late position play. Remember though that if the raise came from someone highly likely to have a strong holding (maybe an under-the-gun raise or a tight player from middle position) then you should be much more inclined to just fold.

Raising from the Blinds

As far as raising or reraising out of the blinds with limpers in the pot, you want to be somewhat more cautious. You aren't likely to raise anyone out and you are going to be out of position after the flop. Still you don't want to raise just the top tier hands (AA-QQ and AK), so you might want to occasionally pop a hand like AQs or AJs with a few limpers just to keep them guessing. Be sure to play them like you have a big hand since a lot of people will be putting you on one. You can also make some value raises with good drawing hands and a lot of limpers just like you would in late position.

Preflop Conclusion

Remember that these recommendations should serve only as a starting point. Nothing in poker is concrete; there are no hard-and-fast rules. Use the basic preflop concepts I have given you here to adapt your play to fit table conditions. Learn which types of hands work in which types of pots and use that to your advantage.

Also remember to play the hands that are comfortable for you. If you don't feel that your post-flop play is good enough to play all of the hands I gave you profitably then feel free to throw some of the weaker ones away. As I mentioned in the chapter on deception you want to play all hands that are break even or better to help disguise your good hands, but don't start playing hands you know to have a negative EV. The small amount of deception gained just isn't worth it.

If, on the other hand, you feel that you are at a table where you are far and away the best player then it might not be bad to add a few hands to the mix. Maybe raise AJ in early position as well and defend your big blind a little more. If you do decide to add more hands try raising more. Limping for one bet a little more might be all right as well, but don't go cold-calling many raises. That is one of the biggest leaks you can develop and one of the worst plays you see inexperienced players frequently make.

Always play within your comfort zone and develop your own table image (more on that in a bit) over time. If you are too worried about whether or not a hand is profitable preflop then you won't be able to play it correctly after the flop. Most poker players who first start making a serious effort to improve read a lot of books and begin to play very tight. This is good for a time, but allow yourself to grow. As you start to win more maybe experiment with a couple more hands here and there. If you find yourself playing too many hands then cut back a bit. Your poker game will evolve over time; let it do so naturally, especially with your preflop play, and you will find yourself getting better every day.

Flop Play

Hold'em, like life itself, has its defining moment. It's the flop. When you see the flop, you're looking at 71 percent of your hand, and the cost is only a single round of betting.

—Lou Krieger

On the flop, three cards come on the board at once, making this street the biggest change you will have to endure in a hand of Hold'em. Great hands like pocket aces can turn to rubbish while 7 2 off suit can flop a full house. Whereas before the flop, very few hands are worse than a four- or five-to-one underdog, now hands can easily be drawing entirely dead or very close to it.

All of that makes the flop harder to play and harder to teach than the preflop betting round. Now there are too many possible hands and too many factors that must be taken into account to come up with hard and fast rules like we could preflop. The good news is that there are a number of common situations we can address that should give you a pretty good outline of what to do.

On the flop, just as on the round before, you should be playing relatively tight. What this means is that if your hand misses the flop you should be throwing it away. If you limp in a multi-way pot with a hand like:

and the flop hits:

you are going to fold if anyone bets. A lot of weaker players might try to chase a runner-runner diamond draw but the odds against that (roughly 25-1 against) are so large as to make that play almost invariably unprofitable.

Aggressive Play

On the flop, it is of utmost importance to play aggressively if you flop a hand that is likely the best. If your hand is:

and the flop hits:

you are highly likely to have the best hand. Now you want to bet and raise to narrow the field. The preflop betting has put numerous bets in the pot and you want to protect your hand.

Most of the times you think your hand has a good shot at being the best hand, you want to play it aggressively. And by the best hand, I mean the hand that is currently the highest ranking, not necessarily the hand that has the best chance of winning. Some very big drawing hands might actually be favorites over made hands, but more on that in a minute.

Three Types of Hands

There are three types of hands you can flop: made hands, drawing hands, and trash hands. Made hands are ones that have a good shot of being the best hand currently and winning the pot unimproved. Drawing hands are hands that probably aren't the best right now but have a chance to become the best hand on a later street. Trash hands are the ones that have little or no chance of being the best and about the same shot of becoming the best.

Trash Hands

I won't spend much time on trash hands because for the most part you should just be folding them. If you see a flop with:

and the board comes:

your beautiful preflop hand has now turned into a pile of garbage. Anyone with an ace or a nine has you very nearly drawing dead.

One of the biggest mistakes you will see poor players often make is continuing on with a hand like this passively. Often they do it because their hand seemed very valuable to them preflop. KQs is a pretty hand, especially after a long run of poor starting hands, so it may be hard to part with it on the flop. Don't let yourself do this. If the flop comes badly for your hand accept reality and don't find yourself check-calling it out.

If the flop completely misses you then you are left with two options. You can either just give up and check/fold the hand or try to bluff the pot. What you should do depends on a number of factors, such as how many players are in, what you put them on, how likely you think they are to fold, what they did preflop, what cards are on the board, etc.

The more opponents you have the less likely you are to be able to bluff the pot and the more likely you should therefore just give up and fold. Also, the higher the cards on the board the more likely you should be to just give up as well. This is because people tend to play higher cards so there is a much greater likelihood that someone flopped top pair if the flop comes ace high than there is if it comes 7 high.

My general rule of thumb is not to bluff at more than two people. If you have three or more opponents you want to at least have some outs to semi-bluff with. Chances are that against three or more players you are going to get at least one call and you are committing yourself to follow through on the turn and maybe even the river.

Also I am much less inclined to bluff on flops with an ace or a king. A lot of people play many hands containing those two cards so the odds of being up against a made hand are much higher. I might semi-bluff with big cards like that on board but just running a flat out bluff with little chance of making the best hand becomes much harder to do.

In general, most of the times you flop no hand and no draw you should give up. This is especially true against loose/weak competition. They are much more likely to call you down with marginal holdings (perhaps ace-rag in the above example) so your bluff is much less likely to succeed. They are also the sort of people who might check to you on the flop and give you a chance to pick up a hand or a draw on the turn for free.

Nonetheless if you do decide to continue on with the hand do so aggressively. You are going to need to make everyone fold, and they can't do that if you are checking and calling. You don't necessarily have to start betting or raising on the flop if you think that it might be more convincing to just check or call the flop and bet or raise the turn, but you should at least be formulating your plan ahead of time. Don't check and call just trying to hit something; either fold your hand or start planning and/or executing your bluff.

Made Hands

Made hands are ones which you think have a good shot of being the best hand and can win the pot without improvement. It is important to note that some hands that may appear to be made hands are actually drawing hands or even trash hands. Figuring out which category your hand rightfully belongs in is a very important part of the game and one that you will generally get much better at with experience. Still, there are a couple easy rules to help you as you learn.

Generally, top pair is considered a pretty decent made hand, especially if it has a good kicker. That is not to say that a lower pair can't be a good hand, but on most flops what you are really looking for is top pair or better. This is very dependent on the texture of the board, however. A hand like:

on a flop that looks like:

looks to be a very strong hand. Here you have top pair with the highest possible kicker on a raggedy board. None of your

opponents are likely to be playing anything like queen-six or six-two and you probably would have heard about it preflop if anyone had something like pocket kings or aces. So your hand might look to be very strong.

Some top pairs are not so powerful. If you see a free flop from the big blind with a hand like:

and the flop hits:

your top pair might be in very bad shape. People would often play bigger kings or hands like Q J, AT, or 9T suited. Even if your hand is the best someone can easily have 8 or more outs just by having a spade or a ten so your hand has a high chance of being drawn out on.

Also the larger the top pair the better it is. If you flop a pair of aces, then nobody can beat you by just pairing one card; they have to hit at least two pair. If you flop a pair of tens, even if it is the best hand, any jack, queen, king, or ace can potentially give someone a better hand. Having a kicker that is higher than your top pair can help cut this effect down a bit. If you hold JQ and the flop hits jack high an opponent can't outdraw you by hitting a pair of queens. Still it is much better to flop a pair of aces to begin with.

An overpair, or a pair higher than any of the cards on the board, is a much better hand than top pair. If you hold:

and the flop hits:

you are probably in great shape since anyone with a hand like AJ is probably going to be willing to put in a decent amount of money with it. Like with top pairs the bigger the overpair the better, and for the same reason. This is part of why bigger pairs are so much more valuable than smaller ones, because even if a hand like 77 is an overpair on the flop, there are a lot of cards that can come on the turn or river to change that.

Two pair on the flop is even better yet. Like with one pair, the more ragged the flop the better. Of course the better your two pair in relation to the board the better your hand is. And again the higher in rank they are the better since it makes it harder for your opponent to catch a higher two pair.

Anything above two pair on the flop is a very strong hand. A straight or a flush is very rare on the flop and should be considered a very valuable holding. Of course keep the

board in mind. Flopping a straight with:

on a board that looks like:

is vastly preferable to doing so with a board of:

because the chances of being drawn out on or having been outflopped are much higher in the second scenario. The same holds true with flopping flushes. A 3-high flush on the flop, while still probably the best hand, can easily lose to a bigger flush if a fourth card of that suit comes. A king-high flush is much more likely to remain the best hand.

Sets (three of a kind using a two from your hand and one from the board) are very strong hands on the flop as well, but trips (three of a kind using one card from your hand and two from the board) are much tougher to play. Even with trips your hand is probably the best, especially if you have a good kicker, but if it isn't you can be drawing fairly slim. Pay a lot of attention to your opponents to see if they have a better one. They may of course try to deceive you as well so don't let them trick you into putting in a lot of raises on the turn or river with a dominated hand.

Anything above a flush is a monster. You will flop full houses and lose sometimes, but it will be rare. I have probably played nearly a half a million hands of Hold'em and have yet to flop four of a kind or better and lose the pot, though I have seen it happen once or twice. With a hand that good your primary consideration is just how to get the most money in the pot. That is where slowplaying should be a consideration, but even then you often stand to make the most money in the long run by simply leading out on the flop.

How to Play Made Hands

With made hands you are, for the most part, going to want to play your hand fast on the flop. I talked about slowplaying already but as you might remember from that chapter I recommend using it very sparingly. At least 95 percent of the time you flop a good made hand, you are going to want to play it aggressively. I advocate doing a lot of betting on the flop. That doesn't mean that you always have to bet, you should often consider check-raising as well, but most of the time you flop a hand you think is the best, you should just lead right out. Make that the staple of your flop play and add check-raising in for variety.

Which play you should choose depends on what happened preflop. Who was in the pot with you? How strong is your hand? What position are you in? If you flop a true

monster, maybe something like

on a board of:

you will probably want to get as much money in on the flop as possible. Let's say you defended the big blind against a button raise with 3 other limpers in the pot before the flop. You might want to lead out here and hope to get some calls and a raise behind you so you can reraise. Your hand is very strong and you want to charge your opponents as much as you can to continue on, especially since most of the good draws they can have will only split the pot with you if they hit. This is the kind of flop where a lot of them are going to draw at you no matter what you do (and are highly likely to raise) so try to get them to dump in as much as you can.

Now if you had the same hand with the same exact pre-flop action but the flop came:

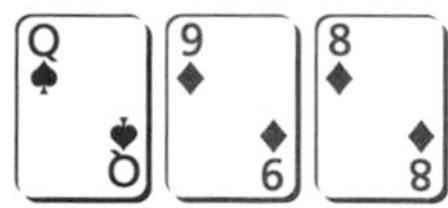

you might want to try to check-raise the late position raiser.

Here you have a hand that is very fragile (if it is the best hand), so you would like to try to make all of those preflop limpers face a double bet in order to convince them to fold hands with a ten or a jack.

In either case you want to play very aggressively. Make people fold or take as poor odds as possible to draw at you. Only check-raise if you are fairly sure that someone will bet, especially if the pot is large. The larger the pot the higher the danger of giving a free card, so keep that in mind.

Because I advocate playing a very aggressive, very positional game preflop you are often going to find yourself in short-handed pots or at least in late position. Late position makes it easy because you don't have to even consider check-raising. Short-handed pots, especially if they have been thinned because you opened with a raise, are also easy because you will mainly just want to bet as well. Check-raising is fine when you have a few players behind you who can bet and you didn't show much aggression before the flop. When you raise preflop and get one caller, checking to him on the flop may look suspicious enough for him to check and take a free turn, so you are almost always better off just leading out.

When You Think You Might Be Beat

When you have a hand that you think has a good shot of being the best hand but you aren't sure you should play aggressively, especially if the pot is large. If your hand is the

best you do yourself a great service by protecting it. If your hand is not the best you still might actually have a higher EV by narrowing the field down to you and the better hand than you would by playing it passively. The larger the pot and the more chance there is that your hand is the best, the more you should lean towards playing it aggressively. If the pot is smaller and/or you think you have less chance of your hand being the best then you might want to consider just letting it go, especially if you think that your opponent might have a good draw if he doesn't have you beat. Remember that from the chapter on semi-bluffing?

When You Are Way Ahead or Way Behind

There is one situation in Hold'em where I will flop a made hand and play it passively. That is when I flop a hand that is either way ahead or way behind. Suppose a late-middle position player (maybe two or three spots before the button) opens with a raise and you defend your big blind with a hand like:

Let's say the flop comes:

Chances are here that your opponent either has you drawing

to a three outer (if he has a bigger ace) or a runner-runner (if he flopped a set) or he himself is drawing to very few outs or even a runner-runner. If he has a bigger ace and you get aggressive it is easy for him to raise you a couple times and force you to put a good amount of money in the pot. If he has something like KQs it is easy for him to get away from it. Either case is bad for you.

In a situation like this you should consider check-calling. Note that this isn't a slowplay because you aren't planning on getting aggressive later. You would very much like to just check-call the whole way and let him bluff with something. Your feigned weakness may entice him to put in some bets thinking he can steal the pot with a hand that is drawing very slim. And if he has you beat you could very well save yourself some money. So you may stand to make more when he doesn't have you beat and lose less when he does, which is a win-win situation for you.

Drawing Hands

Drawing hands are a much different consideration than made hands. What you should do with them depends on how likely your draw is to hit, how likely your draw is to win if it hits, how much you will have to spend to draw, and how big the pot will be when you win. Much of determining what you should do with a drawing hand goes back to the mathematics explained in the chapters on mathematics in the beginning of this book. I won't talk too much about the math since it is already covered there, but be sure you understand it.

There are all sorts of different draws and you will need to know the odds against hitting each. On the flop you have two cards left to come, so be sure to consider your implied odds in your calculations. If you draw at something like a flush and don't hit the turn you may have to call a big bet there to see the river. Count that into your equations.

Most of the math involved comes down to knowing your chances of hitting whatever it is you are drawing at. This can be accomplished by simple memorization. You will often find yourself drawing with the same number of outs, such as nine for a flush draw, eight for an open-ended straight draw, or four for a gutshot straight draw. Know the odds of hitting those common draws with one or two cards left to come.

I have an appendix giving the odds against hitting on the turn, river, or the two combined in the back of this book as a reference for you to use in the future. It might help you to look at these odds when reviewing hands after a session that you have played. Even if you aren't mathematically inclined and have a hard time calculating the odds while sitting at the table, you can always examine them later using a calculator if need be. That may help when similar situations arise in the future.

With drawing hands implied, odds become very important. The odds of your hitting a flush draw on the turn are just over 4-1 against. However if you hit the turn you may be able to win a few bets from your opponents so you would probably need a little less than 4-1 to make the call. The same is true with any draw. A gut-shot straight draw is nearly 11-1 against hitting on the turn but if it comes it might be well disguised, so you might be able to get a good amount of money in the pot afterward. You can use the equations in the section on mathematical expectation to determine exactly what odds you need for the call to be correct.

Common Types of Draws

For the most common draws, four-flush and open ended straight draws, your odds of hitting are roughly 2-1 against with two cards left to come, meaning that you have about a 1/3 shot of hitting. These aren't exact odds but they are close enough to use at the table. Let's assume you limped on the button behind three other limpers and the small blind folds. The big blind checks and you take a flop five-handed. Suppose you hold:

and the flop hits something like:

There are five players in the pot, including yourself, making the average hand a 1/5 shot to win. Your hand has about a one-in-three shot of hitting an ace high flush here so we will say that you have a roughly one-in-three shot of winning. We are ignoring the possibilities of hitting an ace or running 7's

for three of a kind and the possibility of hitting a flush and losing to a full house and just calling it a 1/3 shot for simplification.

Let's say the big blind bets out and all three limpers call. Now you might want to consider raising. Now if you raise and everyone calls you have netted yourself a little extra EV over just calling. If, however, the big blind sand everyone else folds you have cost yourself a little EV since you got the pot down to two-handed (giving the average hand a 1/2 shot of winning) but you only have a 1/3 shot.

Whether you decided to raise or call should depend on how likely you are to get reraised in the situation above. In that situation, you had good relative position; in most you will not. If you were instead the player UTG (therefore acting directly after the big blind) you would almost certainly never raise since you would then force all of the people behind you to face a double bet, almost ensuring that you see the turn heads up. It's better to just call and let everyone trail in behind you.

Draw Strengths

It is very important to always consider the relative strength of your draw. This is because a draw can be very expensive if you hit it and lose the pot anyway. For this reason a hand like:

on a board of:

is a much stronger hand than a hand like:

on a board like

In the first example if you hit your flush an opponent would have to have two clubs in his hand, one of them a king or an ace, to beat you. In the second example if you hit a flush an opponent need only hold the king or the ace of clubs and any other card, making the odds of an opponent having a better hand many times more likely.

Open-ended straight draws are also much more powerful when two of the straight cards are in your hand. If you hold:

and the flop hits:

you have a very good open ended draw. Either a king or an eight gives you a hand that can only be tied, and the odds of someone else holding that same Q J are slim. If on the other hand you have:

and the flop hits:

your open end is much less powerful. Now a king or an eight will have to split the pot with anyone else who has a queen, and someone with AQ will win the entire pot if a king hits.

Overcards

What about when you have a hand like KQ and the flop

comes all rags? Now you have two cards higher than the board but no pair. How you should play a hand like this will depend greatly on the situation. If the pot is short-handed, the flop is extremely ragged, and you had the initiative preflop (maybe you raised and the blind defended) you might try to semi-bluff with it on the flop. If there are a lot of people in the pot and someone else had raised preflop you might just be better off giving up.

Many weak players have a tendency to take overcards way too far. Try to remember that they are a rather poor holding. Even if you are drawing live you only have six outs. If an opponent has a pair with a kicker that matches one of the cards in your hand you may only be drawing at three outs. And if he has two pair or better you may be drawing very slim indeed.

So be careful not to lump overcards in as a drawing hand when they are not. If you find it even remotely possible that your opponents might have two pair or better you are probably better off just giving up. If, however, the pot is pretty decent sized and nobody appears to have much you might be okay taking one card off and seeing what comes.

Overcards are much more powerful when combined with something else. For instance if you are holding that same KQ and the flop comes something like T92 rainbow, you now have a much stronger hand. You can hit a jack for the nut straight, giving you four outs to the nuts; a king or a queen may be enough good to win as well. The more likely

you think a king or queen will win it for you, the stronger your hand is.

Partial Outs

When examining whether or not to continue with overcards, whether you have other outs or not, it is very useful to count your partial outs. Partial outs are cards that may or may not win the pot for you. If you think in our above example that hitting your king or queen (of which there are six total) will win for you half of the time then count them as three outs total. So you would count your hand as basically a seven-outer, since you have four outs to the nuts that you know are good and you are counting your six partial outs as three total. If you thought there was a 75 percent shot of the king or queen being good then you would count those six partial outs as 4.5 (6 * 0.75) total outs so your hand would then count as an 8.5-outer.

Also consider any runner-runner flush possibilities to add up to one out, since a runner-runner flush has about the same chance of hitting as a one outer. This assumes that you have two of the flush suit in your hand and one on the board. If you have one of the flush suit and two on the board then you shouldn't count anything other than the ace of that suit as one out since there is too much chance of getting there and losing. Trying to catch a bad flush with four of the suit on the board is financial suicide.

Semi-bluffing

As I mentioned earlier, semi-bluffing is a very powerful play in Hold'em. Not only is it immediately profitable in many cases, but it also helps disguise your good hands. You can't simply bet all of your made hands and then check-call all of your draws and check-fold all of your junk hands. Then anytime you bet, your opponents will know that you have a hand. So in order to prevent this you should semi-bluff with good draws a decent amount of the time on the flop.

Semi-bluffing can be done by betting or by check-raising. You should do most of it by simply betting, since that is what you will do with most of your made hands as well, but you must also do a small amount of semi-bluff check raising just to keep your opponents guessing. Flush draws, straight draws, and even overcards can all be excellent hands to semi-bluff with. Remember that the more outs you have, the less chance you need to steal immediately for a semi-bluff to be profitable.

Of course, the fewer opponents in the pot, the greater your odds of stealing, so the more you should semi-bluff. Also the lower the board cards are, the less likely it is that one of your opponents will call. The exception to this is certain times when an ace flops. Often your opponents' preflop actions will indicate to you that they have a weak hand. Maybe they just limped in middle position after everyone folded to them, or maybe they limped in late position with

only one limper already. Strong players would probably have raised an ace in either of those positions.

Furthermore, the ace makes it very hard for opponents to call with weak holdings; if they don't have a pair, they know that they will have to get two pair or better to beat anyone who does have an ace. Even if they have a smaller pair, an ace is very scary to them because a lot of people see flops with an ace in their hand. So you might want to semi-bluff in certain situations where you flop an open-end or a four-flush and there is an ace on the board. If you are wrong and someone lets you know that they have an ace, at least you have outs.

The Free Card

With drawing hands, it is sometimes advisable to try to get what is called a free card. This is when you raise the flop with the intention of checking the turn if you miss. This saves you a small bet over calling on both the flop and turn. Consider the above example where you flopped an ace-high flush draw on the button and there was a bet and three calls before you. If you raise and everyone calls they are highly likely to check to you on the turn. If something like the 3 of clubs hits the turn and everyone checks you can then opt to check behind them and get a free river card. Your raise on the flop might have saved you from having to call a bet on the turn.

Note that if you raise for a free card and hit the turn, you might actually have made yourself an extra bet or two on the flop. Now you can just go ahead and bet the turn.

Unfortunately, if they did just call the flop and check to you on the turn, you might have missed an opportunity to raise on the turn as now they are highly likely to just check-call since the flush came.

Jamming the Pot With Draws

Another thing to remember is that if your hand is more likely to win than the average hand remaining in the pot, you want to get as much money in as possible. So if there are four people, including you, remaining in the pot (implying the average hand would have a one-in-four shot of winning), but your draw has a one-in-three shot of hitting, you would want all of your three opponents to put in as much as possible. This is pretty easy to see if you use the equation from the EV section. Remember though that if your attempts to get that money in the pot drive two of the hands out you now have a one-in-three shot of winning the pot—but the average chance of winning is now one-in-two, so you have actually hurt yourself. You want to keep your opponents in while stringing them along for as many bets as possible.

Made and Drawing Hands

Sometimes you flop a hand that could be both a made hand and a drawing hand. An example might be when you have:

and the flop hits:

Now you have a true monster. Your hand is fairly likely to be the best hand, and even if it isn't, it may have a lot of outs. The only hand that is really a significant favorite over the above hand would be a set, and even then you would have just shy of a one-in-three shot of winning. With hands like this just get as much money into the pot as you can.

Flop Summary

As you can see, for the most part, on the flop you should either be playing aggressively or letting go of your hand. There are certainly some exceptions, but for the most part you want to be playing what is known as "fit or fold" poker. Don't make the rookie mistake of continuing on with few or no outs after the flop. Don't call a lot of bets with a hand like middle pair in a multi-way pot either. For the most part, if you can't play aggressively you can't play—period.

Of course, there is no rule that says you can only be aggressive with solid made hands. In fact if you do, your observant opponents will have too much of a read on you. In order to keep your opponents guessing you should be doing a decent amount of semi-bluffing. This can be accomplished by betting. It can also be accomplished by raising or check-raising, though in those cases you will often have to follow up with a turn bet even if you don't improve.

With made hands, you generally want to play aggressively. Even if you think you may be beat, you still might want to get the pot down to you and the better hand. If the flop hits you, then eliminate as many drawing hands as you can and charge the rest dearly to draw at you.

Since you want to charge drawing hands as much as possible when you have a made hand it should be no surprise that when you have a drawing hand you want to be charged the least amount possible. In general you will want to play your hand passively (except when semi-bluffing of course) and keep as many opponents in as possible while keeping the bet cheap. The exception to this is when your draw has an above average chance of winning the pot and you can get everyone to put in more money. Situations like that aren't exceedingly common, but they do happen so be sure to take advantage of them when they do.

As with all of poker much of what you do on the flop should be based on what you know of your opponents and what happened on the previous betting round. Always keep in mind that different situations call for different actions. You must constantly adjust your play depending on what the board brings or what your opponents do. Sometimes top pair is a very strong hand; sometimes two pair is a weak one. It all depends on the flop.

Turn Play

It's hard work. Gambling. Playing poker. Don't let anyone tell you different. Think about what it's like sitting at a poker table with people whose only goal is to cut your throat, take your money, and leave you out back talking to yourself about what went wrong inside. That probably sounds harsh. But that's the way it is at the poker table. If you don't believe me, then you're the lamb that's going off to the slaughter.

—Stu Ungar

The turn is probably the most important street in limit Hold'em. Here is the round where you will make your most critical decisions. Good play on the turn is much of what separates the good players from the bad, the big winners from the small. It is the first street to feature the larger bet, which is double the size of the bet on the round before. Unlike the river, which also features a double bet, there is still a card left to come so we have many more considerations than we do on the last street.

On the turn players tend to give a much better indication as to the strength of their hand than they do on the flop. There usually isn't any sense slowplaying a hand past the turn (though you frequently see poor players do so), so all of

the slowplayers will generally spring their trap. The bet is now as big as it is ever going to get, so for the most part they try to get as much out of you as they can immediately.

Making Big Laydowns

The turn is the street in Hold'em where you should be making most of your best laydowns. If someone bets at you on the turn and you have a made hand, then you have to call a big bet there and potentially one on the river as well. This can give you very poor implied odds. So the turn is the one street where, when in doubt, you should probably lean towards folding if an opponent gets aggressive. As with all decisions (and I'm sure you're sick of hearing this by now) it depends on a lot of factors, implied odds, your opponents, all of that stuff.

On the flop you can take a lot of speculative holdings to the next round because the bet is so cheap and if you make a strong hand you have two rounds of double bets to get paid on it. On the river you probably only have to call one big bet to see if your hand is good and are getting great odds to do so. On the turn, however, it is a much different story. You are facing a big bet, which makes your direct pot odds often worse than they were on the flop.

Also, your implied odds are often much worse since you might have to call a big bet on both the turn and the river. Furthermore, you only have one round of betting left to capitalize if you make a big hand. Because there are no more

cards to come on the river (meaning that knocking people out has much less value), people tend to play much more passively there as well; you become less likely to get a lot of bets out of someone.

So the turn is the one street in Hold'em where we often must give folding some serious thought if we have a good hand. Preflop you pretty much know what to play and what not to play; the decisions are mostly fairly easy. On the flop the decisions become a bit tougher, but as long as you aren't drawing dead even a bad call is generally a big mistake. And as we will see in the next chapter, your decision is fairly easy on the river as well.

Of course, good turn play, like every other part of the game, comes with experience. Just keep in mind your odds, both direct and implied, and how they are affected by the double bet. And remember that there is no prize in Hold'em for having had the best hand on the flop. If the turn comes bad for your hand and it appears to have you beat, then there is no sense putting in more money, unless of course you have the odds to draw for an even better hand on the river.

Follow Through

One of the most important things to understand about turn play is that you should generally follow through on your flop betting. If you bet a made hand on the flop and were called, you should generally bet it again on the turn. It might be scary if you bet top pair and an overcard or a flush comes,

but unless you are very certain you are beat, you should bet again. You can't risk giving free cards. If a bad card comes and you get raised then you have a tough decision to make, but don't fall into the rookie mindset of slowing down every time a bad turn card comes.

Part of the reason for this is that opponents will call with a lot of speculative hands on the flop while the bet is cheap. When the bet increases on the turn, it can be much harder for them to continue. Opponents will be much more likely to give up on hands like middle pair or a gutshot, especially if you had bet the flop.

You should generally also continue with your bluffs and semi-bluffs. Again, your opponents might have been calling the flop with something a little more speculative and may now be inclined to just let you have it. Betting the turn also makes your river bluff more likely to succeed should it come to that as a player who bets all three rounds often appears to have a real hand. So even if your turn bluff doesn't succeed, the attempt may help you sell one on the river.

Bluffing and Semi-Bluffing

In addition to following up on your flop semi-bluffs, you can add some new semi-bluffs on the turn. Maybe an opponent bet at you on the flop and you called with a flush draw. If he checks the turn you might want to bet since it could look to him like you had a mediocre hand on the flop and weren't sure if it was good. Since he checked the turn he probably

can't beat the mediocre hand you are representing and he may fold.

You can also mix in some plain old bluffs as well. Let's say you checked on the big blind with two opponents behind you and the flop came king-high. You have rags in your hand and check, and so do the other two players. If the turn is a blank you might want to bet out with your rags, pretending that you just had a weak king or a second pair on the flop and weren't sure if it was good.

As with bluffing on any street, it is very important to sell your bluffs on the turn. If your bet appears to be a bluff your opponents will be highly likely to call you down. If it appears to actually be a hand then they will be more inclined to fold. Before bluffing it is often good to think about what hands your opponent can put you on that will make them fold. If there aren't at least a few you are probably better off not trying. If there are a lot of them then go ahead and give it a whack.

Drawing Hands

Drawing hands that hit the turn should be played aggressively, almost without exception. If you call with a gutshot and you hit it, then you better raise. The same is true with a flush draw or anything else you were drawing at. If you can't raise whatever you hit, then you probably shouldn't have been drawing at it in the first place. The bet doesn't get any bigger on the river, so why wait?

The only exception to this is if you hit a card that makes

your draw and might make someone else a better one. For instance, if the turn card gives you a flush but pairs the board. In that case if the pot gets jammed you have to make a tough decision about whether or not you are beat. Just because you hit a good hand doesn't mean you have to call a lot of bets with it. If it looks pretty sure to be beat, now is the time to lay it down.

If your drawing hand from the flop misses the turn now you will have to make another decision. Again, consider your pot odds and the odds against your hitting on the river. Be sure to factor in any bets you expect to receive should you hit your hand as well. Count partial outs the same way that you did on the flop.

Many times a hand that has the odds to draw on the flop does not have the odds on the turn. This happens often with hands like gutshot straight draws that just barely have the odds to call on the flop. It can also happen with a flush or straight draw as well, though it will usually take a raise to make you fold it. Don't be afraid to let go of a drawing hand if the odds just aren't there anymore. Sure, sometimes you will fold it and the draw will hit, but pay attention only to your EV and ignore short-term results.

Also, be careful when drawing at hands like straights or flushes on a paired board. If the pot gets jammed it might often be correct to fold even if you think you have the odds to call just because of the chance that you make your hand and don't win. If someone has three of a kind on a paired

board then as many as three of your flush outs might also make them a full house (two that pair the board and one that pairs their kicker) and you might not know what one of them is. Also, if you think there is a good chance someone already has a full house then you are drawing dead, and that is very expensive on the turn.

River Play

Last night I stayed up late playing poker with Tarot cards.
I got a full house and four people died.
—Steven Wright

The river is, in many respects, very easy to play. As I mentioned earlier, there are only two reasons to bet once all of the cards are dealt: to make a player with a better hand fold, and to make a player with a worse hand call. All of the other considerations go out the window, so on the river we only have to consider two factors when deciding whether or not to bet. Bluff or bet for value. If you can't do either then check and/or fold.

Please keep in mind though that just because you know this doesn't mean your opponents always do. In higher-limit games most people at least intrinsically understand this principle, but at a lot of lower-limit games, you will run into players who bet hands that aren't likely to bluff out a better hand and aren't likely to get called by a worse one. Be aware of players like that and adjust your game accordingly. But against good players remember that they know why they should bet, and use that to help get a read on them.

Value Betting

Whether to value bet is often a tough decision but one with limited consequences. A successful value bet adds one big bet to your overall win. In a game where you are expecting to make one or two big bets per hour, it is easy to see that an extra value bet or two every night can have a significant impact on your rate. That is why I recommend value betting somewhat liberally on the river, especially against opposition that is prone to making weak turn calls. But even if your extra value bets succeed two out of three times (a good rate) it may only add up to one extra big bet per night, and that is assuming that none of them get raised. That is great, don't get me wrong, but it isn't going to make the difference between a loser and a winner, or if it does you need to work on your play more on the first three streets.

Against better players who are less prone to call the turn with weaker holdings you are going to want to be more selective about value betting, especially if they are the sort to bluff induce a lot. Chances are they were either drawing and missed (in which case they will just fold on the river and your value bet gains nothing) or had a good hand. If you are pretty sure that they have a hand but your hand is better then by all means bet, but if you were betting a marginal hand on the turn you might want to just flip it over on the river and see if it was good.

If your hand is marginal or weak and you are out of position, you may often be better off trying to check and call.

With a hand like ace high you generally don't want to bet even if you think it is good. If your opponent has king high or worse, he is probably just going to fold. If he has anything better there is a good chance he will call. In this case, you either win nothing extra (the pot was yours anyway) or you lose one bet.

That is where you might consider bluff inducing. If you check your weak holding your opponent might feel that he can take the pot off of you and you can then call him, netting an extra bet if you are correct. And if he does have you beat, he might just check, saving you a bet. Whether or not to do this depends on your opponent. You have to consider how likely he is to bet a worse hand (a lot of which depends on how he played and whether he feels he can sell a bluff) or how likely he is to check a better hand, and how likely he would be to call if you have a better hand.

This also will help prevent your opponents from bluffing at you later. You can't simply fold every time you check or you are giving your opponents license to walk all over you. Checking and calling (and check-raising) make your opponents think before betting, and when an opponent thinks he can make a mistake. If you always fold after checking he can bet automatically and will therefore never make a mistake.

Also consider the value you give someone when you bet. If you bet a hand and it is the best, your opponent can fold (netting you nothing) or call (netting you one). If he has a better hand (assuming you have a hand and will call if he raises) then he can either call (and you lose one bet) or raise (and you lose 2). You are basically laying him odds and depending on how likely he is to fold a worse hand or raise a better hand this can mean that your value bet must be successful a much higher percentage of the time to show a long term profit.

As far as check-raising for value goes, use this one sparingly. Remember that an opponent is far more likely to raise the river (allowing you to threebet) than he is to threebet against your check raise. Also remember that with marginal hands in position on the river, opponents are much more likely to just roll their hands over and see if they win without giving you a chance to check-raise. And of course don't forget that you are giving your opponents an overlay, just as you are by betting.

Still, a check-raise, when it works, can net you an extra bet or more. If you bet and an opponent calls but you could have check-raised (assuming he calls that) you lost a bet. So if you think there is better than a 50 percent chance of gaining an extra bet by check-raising then go for it.

A very typical time to check-raise is when you hit a flush or a straight on the river. You will see a lot of opponents do this all the time. Against players like that if they appear to have been drawing you must consider checking even decent hands against them. As you move up in limits you will notice that better players are much more inclined to often just bet out when they hit a draw, especially flushes since they are much more obvious, but at limits $15/$30 and below be much more wary of people check-raising draws.

Against more aware opposition the best times to check-raise the river are the ones where your hand is more disguised, such as a straight or a runner-runner flush. Let's say you defend the big blind against a raise and a caller from the small blind. You have:

and semi-bluff on a flop of:

with a gutshot. You bet out wanting to see what the raiser does and get raised. The small blind folds and you are getting 9-1 and decide you have the odds to take one card off so you call. On the turn the board looks like:

giving you a flush draw as well and you check-call. Now since the board was raggedy on the flop if you think your opponent has a good hand (maybe AK or something) it might look to him as if you are check-calling with a weaker hand, probably a weak ace, making him very inclined to bet on the river. So if the river looks like:

you may want to consider a check-raise. If you bet there is a very good chance that your opponent will be scared into just calling with his ace. If he was bluffing, he may just fold. If you check though he will probably continue a bluff if he is on one or value bet with is ace if he has that. In either case you make one more bet.

Bluffing The River

If you were bluffing or semi-bluffing the whole way, then you will probably want to continue to do so on the river if you failed to improve. If you have no shot of winning by checking then you might as well give betting a shot. Chances are the pot is good sized so you won't have to win often. You should be especially prone to betting in that case if you think your opponent may have been drawing. So if you bet something like a small flush draw the whole way and miss, then bet the river and hope your opponent was drawing at the same flush and will give you credit for something. If your flush draw was an ace high one though you might be better off checking and hoping it's good since your opponent will probably call you with a pair and fold anything worse.

As far as bluffing goes on the river when you weren't

leading the whole way, only try it when you can sell it. For instance in a $40/$80 game I was playing, I had raised:

in middle position (two spots before the button) in an eight-handed game. Both blinds called and the flop came:

I bet and the small blind check-raised me. The big blind folded and I called. The turn was a six giving me a gutshot too and making the board something like:

My opponent bet and I called again. The river was the ace of diamonds. My opponent checked and I bet. Now that was selling the bluff since it probably looked to him like I had AK or AQ. He figured out that I didn't have an overpair when I just called his raise on the flop and his bet on the turn. He probably also figured that if I had something with a ten in it I would probably just check and try to show it down. Therefore, he was probably putting me on AK since a lot of

people would have called with that. When the river came and I bet he folded, probably thinking I must have hit. There was a good chance he just had a flush draw there too since he probably would have called with a ten, but chances are his flush draw was higher than mine since he called a raise from the small blind with it. Who knows though, he might have had a ten and just been sure he was beaten. In either case I am pretty sure I was beat but my bet won me a $560 pot.

In any case, be sure to bluff a little on the river. If you never bluff your opponents will pick up on that. Then they can simply fold their weak hands any time you bet and bet whenever you don't. Remember that a good bluff is one that succeeds enough of the time to be profitable so even if most of your bluffs fail you might still be doing a great job of it. In fact if most of your bluffs succeed you aren't bluffing enough.

If a bluff does get called consider it part of your advertising budget. You shouldn't bluff specifically for advertisement purposes; you should bluff for profit. But remember that even the ones that fail still have some value since they add deception to your game.

As far as bluff-raising or bluff check-raising go, I advise generally avoiding it. After you have gained experience and are playing at a limit where people are seeking to play well there will occasionally be a situation in which it might be a good play. But generally speaking, you are investing twice as much, wrecking your pot odds and making the play need to succeed a much higher percentage of the time than a bluff bet would. Also to raise or check-raise, an opponent must already have bet, and for the raise to be better than a call he must fold a better hand than yours. Therefore you would only make this play with a hand that has no shot of winning, since even a hand like bottom pair is highly likely to be called by an opponent who had already bet the river. If he folds it is highly likely that your bottom pair was good anyway so your raise gains you nothing.

Calling the River

The decision of whether or not to call another player's bet is generally pretty easy. In general, if you have any shot of winning the pot, you call. Making tough laydowns on the river is not the way to win at limit poker. If the pot is raised and you have to cold call two bets to show down that is another story, but in instances where you have any hand at all and the pot is decent sized, you are probably going to call, especially if there is no chance of it being raised.

This somewhat makes up for the overlay I mentioned when value betting the river earlier. Any good opponent knows that they should call often on the river. If an opponent knew your hand, then you could never value bet the river, since he would just fold when you are beaten and raise when he has you better, giving him an infinite overlay. Of course he doesn't know what you have, and that makes a big difference. Now he has to call a lot of the hands where you have the best holding and fold some of the ones where you are bluffing as well. This keeps the overlay you are really giving him down to a reasonable level where you can still value bet at times.

So remember that the higher the odds you are getting (and when calling on the river we use only direct odds since there are no implied odds) the more likely you should be to call. If you are getting nine to one then you only need for your opponent to be bluffing or value betting a weaker hand one in ten times for a call to show a profit. If your opponent doesn't have a one in ten shot of being on a bluff in most situations then there is probably something wrong with him. In that case you would, of course, fold your weaker hands, but against the vast majority of people the chances of their bluffing will be high enough for you to call most hands of any strength at all on the river.

Also remember that calling on the river shows your opponents that they can't bluff you which is a good thing. You don't want people bluffing at you unless they are the type who do it far too much, in which case they probably won't stop no matter how many times you snap them off. Against most people, though, you want to discourage that sort of play. I recently called a couple people down the whole way in a high stakes game with pocket deuces and won pots. I got nicknamed "The Sheriff," which is a great nickname to have. You would be amazed how everyone, including some very well known players you might have seen on television, stopped bluffing at me and checked me into hands or let me hang around with junk that they could have bluffed me out of the pot with.

Overcalling

By the river the pot is usually short-handed, but sometimes you have multiple opponents. The more opponents there are the higher standards you should have for both value betting and calling. In the above discussion, I have been more or less talking about decisions against one opponent. When there is already a bet and a call the decision becomes a little tougher.

As far as value raising there you need a pretty strong hand to do it. The bettor bet into two players. The more opponents a bettor has, the more likely he feels he is to be called, and therefore, the better his hand probably is. This will be true of your own betting as well. A pot with more than two players is said to be protected for this reason, since the odds of a steal are greatly reduced.

So if a player bets with a high expectation of a call and another player calls then that caller should also have a fairly good hand. This means that you should be much more inclined to fold your weaker hands. Whereas ace high might sometimes snap off a bluff it will rarely pick up a pot that is bet and called on the river. The same is true of small pairs as well.

Notice that I say the caller "should" have a decent hand, not will. Remember to play your opponents. Some people bluff every river and some players will call with as little as ace high routinely, even with players left to act behind them. If you were against a very liberal bettor and a very liberal caller with a good sized pot you may still want to give it a shot with a junky middle pair or something. Remember that you only need it to work a small portion of the time, and the larger the pot the less frequency your call must win to be profitable.

Conclusion

It is best, when in doubt, to check and/or call the river. Value betting is very tough since you are giving your opponent an overlay by doing so, but if a good chance comes up, you should take it. Good value betting comes with experience and is part of what separates a strong winner from a mediocre one, but isn't a big enough factor to turn a significant loser into a winner. And if your previous actions help to sell a bluff on the river, then give it a shot. The pot is usually large enough that the bluff need not be successful very often to show a profit, and even when it fails it has some deception value. And most importantly don't try to make strong laydowns on the river; save those for the turn.

Always keep in mind the two reasons for betting the river. They are to make a better hand fold and to make a worse hand call. If you can't do either of those, then betting is not a good play. Consider bluff inducing with hands that stand to make all worse hands fold and all better hands call.

SECTION III

Advanced Concepts

Introduction to Advanced Concepts

There are some aspects of the game that become more useful as you gain experience. In these final chapters, I am going to go over some of the more advanced concepts in the game, ranging from bluff inducing to playing shorthanded poker. I am going to structure this chapter a bit more loosely as well. Up until now I have been trying to build a solid game plan in the best logical order possible, writing much the way one might write a math book. Each concept has been built upon the ones before it. Now we are at a point where the reader should know all of the basic concepts and have a good foundation, so it's time to do a little tweaking. The following chapters are structured almost like individual articles.

I am going to end with a few thoughts on poker. I know many people who play poker don't realize what goes into playing as a hobby or professionally. Many players are curious about some of the mathematical terms they hear on television or in poker books. I am going to explain them and why there are useful to you as a player.

There is much to winning at poker besides playing well. Good money management can increase your lifetime profits

just as much as learning to bluff induce or spot tells. In this chapter I will talk a little bit more about those logistical concepts which will hopefully, if employed with discipline, make you a lot of money.

NINETEEN

Tells and Telegraphs

He said, "Son, I've made a life out of readin' people's faces, and knowin' what their cards were by the way they held their eyes."

—Kenny Rogers

Everyone has heard the expression "poker face." And everyone knows that having a good poker face means not letting your mannerisms give away your emotions. Since everyone knows what a poker face is, you would think that most poker players would make a concerted effort to put on a good one, but that's not always true.

When a mannerism gives away some information about a player's hand, that is a tell. Some tells are very obvious, such as players swearing when a card they don't like hits the table. Some tells are very subtle, such as a guy who puts his chips in the pot all in one tall stack when he has a hand and puts his chips in by making two equal sized stacks when he doesn't.

Entire books have been written on tells in poker, most notably by Mike Caro. There are many different common tells, all of which can mean different things when exhibited by different people. Whereas one guy might let out a sigh

when he is bluffing another might let out the same sigh when he is betting the nuts. To truly cover individual tells would require another book of the same size as this, but since Mike Caro has done such a fine job of it I will not delve too deeply into them here.

I will say that the best time to spot tells is when cards are dealt. Looking at people, instead of the board, when the flop, turn, or river is placed on the table will give you a lot of clues as to what they have. You will be surprised how many people jump a little when they hit a big hand or give a very small frown when a card they dislike appears.

Tells can be extremely valuable, so you should watch for them. You will notice that all world-class players have intense focus. They are constantly staring at their opponents trying to find anything useful. Of course top players also rarely exhibit tells so at the highest levels it actually becomes a very small part of the game, but at the lowest limits just trying to spot tells can turn a break-even player into a small winner and a small winner into a strong one.

Since tells can give away very valuable information you should seek to eliminate your own tells. There is a very simple basic theory on how to avoid exhibiting any tells of your own. Plainly put, if you always bet in the exact same manner then that manner could not possibly give an opponent any information as to what you hold. Sounds pretty simple, right? It is and it isn't. It is a hard thing to get used to, controlling where you look, your breathing, and all of the other factors, but once you do get used to it it will become second nature.

So when playing in a casino (and this, of course, has no relevance at all when playing online) always try to stack your chips in the pot the same way using the same hand. Try to control your breathing, your posture, where you look (I recommend always keeping your eyes focused on the chips in the center of the table and not looking at your opponent), or anything else you can think of. And try to make it always the same.

A lot of players like to wear sunglasses, and this isn't a bad idea. I don't do it because it strains my eyes, which in turn makes me tired. I just look right down at the center of the felt every time I bet. If you don't think you can restrain yourself, go ahead and put on some shades.

Telegraphs

Telegraphs are slightly different (but perhaps even more common) than tells. Whereas a tell gives an opponent some idea as to what you are holding, a telegraph gives him some idea as to what your next action will be. An example might be a player who grabs enough chips to bet before it is his turn to act. Like tells, different telegraphs might mean different things when exhibited by different people, but there are a number of common ones which are pretty much universal.

The frequency with which you find players who exhibit numerous telegraphs is alarming. Even in a $30/$60 game in Las Vegas, which is a fairly high-stakes game, you will often find that more than half of the table routinely telegraphs their next action. The most common one you see is people who look at their hand preflop then get ready to throw it away. They seem to be anxiously awaiting their turn to pitch their junk hand, oblivious to the fact that their consistently doing so makes it very easy for you to tell when they do have a hand that they are considering playing.

It is for this reason that I and many other poker authors advocate always looking to your left. You don't want to be too blatant about it, since you don't want the people realizing that you are on to them. Just casually glance over at the next few players' hands before making your move, especially preflop.

At first take note of how their telegraph relates to their actions. If a player always bets when he grabs a bunch of chips before it is his turn to act then you have a great telegraph. If whether they grab chips has no relation to what they do then you have nothing. Also look at how they hold their cards; that is another very common way in which a lot of people telegraph their next action. There are certainly others as well, so be on the lookout for them, but those two comprise the vast majority of telegraphs.

Telegraphs are actually fairly useful when you spot them. Preflop they can give you a good idea of what is going to happen. If you are three or four spots from the button but everyone behind you telegraphs a fold you should treat your position as if it were the button. If, on the flop, an opponent behind you grabs chips to bet with, you can consider check-raising a hand you might otherwise have bet with.

Do be sure though to avoid falling for false telegraphs. These are fairly common as well. Some are made intentionally, some unintentionally. A lot of players who want an opponent to check might grab a lot of chips, as if to say that they are going to raise if bet into. If you are observant you will spot when players do such things and know what it means in the future.

Avoid telegraphing your own hand much the same way you avoid tell—by always doing the same thing. When you get dealt your first two cards always hold them in the same manner. Never touch your chips until it is your turn to act, or if you do then always hold the same amount and hold them the same way. If you were shuffling chips before the round, keep shuffling them until it is your turn to act.

Conclusion

Use both tells and telegraphs to your advantage. Getting a little extra information as to what your opponents hold or are planning to do with their hand can only mean extra profits for you. And be certain not to give either away yourself. With both you avoid giving away information by always doing everything the same exact way. You will have to work at this a bit at first, as most people naturally have very bad poker faces (and hands too) but with a little practice you can make yours second nature.

Plugging Leaks

If you're trying to achieve, there will be roadblocks. I've had them; everybody has had them. But obstacles don't have to stop you. If you run into a wall, don't turn around and give up. Figure out how to climb it, go through it, or work around it.

—Michael Jordan

Most of the biggest errors I see at the poker table are caused by people who see a hole in their game and try to fix it the wrong way. They realize that their opponents are gaining an edge on them due to something that they are doing wrong. They want to fix it but they end up doing a bunch of things they know are bad and end up losing more EV from their bad play than they did from the original problem. The ability to find solid ways to fix the leaks in your game is what separates a big winner from a mediocre one. The trick is to always look for long-term solutions to the problem; don't try to plug your holes with bad short-term play.

The most common problem I see in poker is people worrying about being too predictable. They reason that if they are too predictable, their opponents will always know what they have and therefore always play correctly. This is caused by a number of misconceptions. First of all they probably don't know what a range of holdings is and how their opponents go about putting them on one. They think that a good opponent just knows what they have, which is probably brought on by their results-oriented view of their own reading abilities. You already know about the range of holdings since you read my chapter on psychology.

Second, they don't realize that in poker it is often better for your opponents to know what you have than it is to make a play that disguises your hand. I often see players put in a position where they can either play aggressively and announce to the table that they have a hand and just take the pot down or check and keep their opponents guessing but give them free cards to a draw. In this case it often isn't worth the deception to check. They should just bet and take the pot. You would much rather let everyone know what you have and take the pot then keep them guessing but give them loads of extra EV by letting them catch free cards. What they are doing is making a bad short term play in order to correct their long-term problem.

You often see this problem manifest itself preflop in people who just call a raise from middle position with something like pocket kings. They don't realize that even if three-betting kings tells people that they have a good hand their long term profit is still higher that way then letting in a bunch of stragglers. Don't be afraid to announce your hand if doing so is the play with the highest EV. And if you don't want that play to announce your hand then consider three-betting more hands preflop from middle position. Don't make the terrible short-term play of just cold-calling a raise with a big pair, look for a better long-term solution later.

Most problems can't be fixed profitably by short term solutions, especially in the above example. The problem of predictability, one of the hardest to successfully correct, can only be fixed by playing the rest of your game in a way that makes your play consistently unpredictable, not by routinely making bad plays. If people realize that every time you bet you have something, then don't start checking with hands that you should bet since you know free cards can be very expensive. Instead start betting with hands you would normally check. Remember, earlier I said that bluffs only have to succeed a small amount of the time to be a good play. Therefore adding a few extra bluffs into your game, even if they aren't the best ones, will keep your opponents guessing a lot more and won't cost you much if anything.

Also, as far as predictability goes, don't overestimate how predictable you are. A lot of people give themselves and their opponents much more credit for reading ability than they actually deserve. Playing decent poker is going to often allow people to put you on a narrow range of holdings, but as long as the range they are putting you on is wider than the range you can put them on, you are going to win. Focus more on increasing your own reading ability and don't worry too much about being predictable. Most people who will think you easily predictable just have no clue what they are talking about.

Finding the leaks in your game is simply a matter of

observing how your opponents react to you. Do they bet every time you check? If so then you need to check-raise and bluff induce more. If you are already doing plenty of that then they are making a mistake by betting too much, so capitalize on it. Check-raise and bluff induce them more than you would a normal opponent.

Do opponents call you way more than you would like? Try bluffing a bit less and value betting a bit more. If they continue to call you down all the time it will only cost them money. If they notice what you are doing and start to call you less then swing back the other way, bluffing more.

Does everyone fold every time you raise preflop? If so try mixing in a few more raises. Once someone sees you raise 87s in early position you will be amazed at how much more action you get. And if they continue to fold every time you will keep stealing the blinds, and that is fine too. Only the top few hands have an EV higher than a blind steal, so be glad whenever you get them.

This is where poker becomes a very complicated version of rock- paper-scissors. If your opponent keeps throwing out rock you have to keep putting out paper. If he goes scissors you switch to rock. Always try to compensate for your own weaknesses in a long-term fashion, not by trying to make costly short-term adjustments. And always try to capitalize on their weaknesses. If they spot one of your leaks and try to charge you for it, turn it against them.

The luck element of poker makes it infinitely harder

than rock-paper-scissors. If a guy keeps raising you, it could be that he just keeps getting great hands. It could be that he found that you are a pushover. Or it could just be that he is a maniac. Careful study of him and lots of time at the tables will help you determine which it is. Careful study of the game and lots of time at the tables will teach you how to eliminate your own weaknesses and take advantage of his.

Furthermore, you are playing an individual game of rock-paper-scissors with every player at the table. And you are going to end up in lots of multi-way hands too, where opponents have conflicting strengths and weaknesses that you need to avoid or take advantage of. This can make finding the right play very complicated. For a game that never gives you more than three options it is rather complex, isn't it?

Do be sure to try to avoid seeing weaknesses that aren't there. This is hard to do and again comes with experience. I am truly sorry to keep repeating that line, but there really are some things you just have to learn from experience. You wouldn't want a college student reading a book on brain surgery and then repairing your aneurysm. Similarly you can't expect to read a Hold'em book (or a book on chess, go, backgammon, or any other game worth playing) and be an overnight expert.

So play often and as you do, watch your opponents. See how they react to you and each other. You can discover holes in other people's games just by watching their opponents as well as you can your own. But be sure to walk the fine line between discovering flaws and seeing things that aren't there. And always be sure to look for long-term solutions to your own problems. Don't try to plug up a hole in the short-term by making a bad play. Just do the best you can for now and try to make a permanent adjustment to your game afterwards.

Bluff Inducing

Son, no matter how far you travel, or how smart you get, always remember this: Someday, somewhere, a guy is going to come to you and show you a nice brand-new deck of cards on which the seal is never broken, and this guy is going to offer to bet you that the jack of spades will jump out of this deck and squirt cider in your ear. But, son, do not bet him, for as sure as you do you are going to get an ear full of cider.

—Damon Runyon, "The Idyll of Miss Sarah Brown"

In the chapter on betting I gave many reasons for aggressive play. With cards left to come a few of them were reducing an opponent's expectation (even if you don't make it negative), extracting money from a hand that is drawing dead, and getting more money in the pot when your hand is more likely to win than the average hand. With no cards left to come one of the reasons to bet was to get opponents with a worse hand to pay you. Notice that all of these are only accomplished if your opponent calls. Of course there are plenty of other reasons why you would bet and often you don't want your opponent to call, but sometimes you do. So what to do in those cases where you want your opponent to call but you don't think they will? The answer may be to bluff induce.

Bluff inducing is merely acting passively to entice your opponent to bet and intending to call that bet. That bet that you are inducing may be on the current street or sometimes even on a later one. Note that it is different than check-raising because you don't plan to raise the current round if your opponent bets. And it is different than slowplaying because you aren't trying to trap them into a raising war later in the hand.

You can bluff induce on a current street by checking to a player. You can try to induce a bluff on a later street by either checking behind him or by just calling his bet. You can, of course, try to induce someone to bluff on multiple streets as well.

Bluff inducing is especially potent in situations where you either are a big favorite or a big underdog. If you are a big favorite and you bet your opponent could easily fold. If you are a big underdog and bet he could easily raise you. If this is the case then you either gain nothing by betting or lose extra. Let me give an example.

Suppose an aggressive late position player open raises and you call on the big blind with:

and the flop comes:

Chances are that you are either way ahead with your pair of aces or he has a pair of aces with a bigger kicker, putting you way behind. By betting out you allow him to raise you and charge you extra if you are behind or to simply fold if you are ahead. If he raises you then you are put in a tough spot. There may be a better way to play.

Suppose you check. He is probably going to bet just about anything here. If you call and check the turn he is pretty likely to bet again, especially if he holds something like pocket queens. If he is an aggressive enough player he may even think that your weakness meant that you don't have an ace and bluff at you on the river.

Furthermore if he has you beat you remain in the pot with a minimal investment. Your hand is probably too good to fold here against an aggressive player. So by bluff inducing you could minimize your loss when you are beat and maximize your win when you have the best hand. Both of those are very good things.

Remember in poker that your EV is only a function of how much money is in the pot and how much you put into it. It makes no difference where the bet comes from, just how much it is. If an opponent has a flush draw his EV is reduced the same amount by putting in one bet regardless of who bet and who called.

That being said, bluff inducing has a risk associated with it much like check-raising and/or slowplaying. You are risking letting your opponent hit a better hand. If the pot is

sizeable it may often be preferable to simply bet, even if you let your opponent fold a hand that would be unprofitable for him to bet, just because of the chance of him checking. You have to factor in the cost of a free card. The bigger the pot the more a free card costs you.

Bluff inducing is a valuable deceptive tool. When you get someone with it a couple times they really have to give more consideration to checking behind you in the future. This is a good thing for you. Be sure to mix it into your game. Use it mostly when heads up and when the pot is not large. Don't overuse it either, be sure to sometimes just bet out when a bluff induce might work to keep opponents guessing.

Against maniacs bluff inducing will be one of your primary weapons. Most people, when playing against overly aggressive players, tend to become overly aggressive themselves. This is actually good for the maniac as it makes their over-aggressiveness correct since people become so much more willing to raises and reraise marginal hands. I often see tight players just go nuts with marginal holdings against maniacs. The maniac drags down a huge pot with something like top pair and they start swearing to themselves. Don't fall into this trap. Always remember that maniacs get pocket aces or sets on the flop just as often as anyone else.

The trick to playing against maniacs is to do a lot of calling. You have to play aggressively to get the pot down to just you and them, but if you have a marginal hand and are

heads up with a maniac just bluff induce the hell out of him. As long as they will keep betting their underdogs just keep calling. Now if you have a good hand and are pretty sure you have them beat then pound away, but don't catch yourself putting in raise after raise with top pair no kicker.

With your marginal hands just check-call. If they have a good hand you will save yourself a lot. If they have a poor hand you might even make yourself a little extra, since even the toughest maniac will often slow down when they have nothing and someone gets aggressive. Remember that maniacs are actually, in general, more intelligent than the average player. They aren't stupid, and most of them are actually winning players. They aren't going to keep capping away when you obviously have them beat. But they will keep betting when they aren't sure, so calling them down with marginal hands makes it very tough for them to win.

So be careful with bluff inducing, but be sure to make it a weapon in your arsenal. Used correctly it can be a very valuable tool. Be sure not to take too much risk giving away decent sized pots with it, but reserve it for times when it can either save you money if your hand is beaten or make you money if your hand is the best.

Short-Handed Play

There are few things that are so unpardonably neglected in our country as poker. The upper class knows very little about it. Now and then you find ambassadors who have sort of a general knowledge of the game, but the ignorance of the people is fearful. Why, I have known clergymen, good men, kind-hearted, liberal, sincere, and all that, who did not know the meaning of a "flush." It is enough to make one ashamed of the species.

—Mark Twain

When players begin to leave a poker game and the table gets short, the entire chemistry of the game changes. These changes greatly influence proper strategy, both preflop and postflop. Even though most people understand these changes from a theoretical standpoint due to some of the poker books written in the past, very few players, even among those who play professionally, adapt their game correctly when the table gets short. This presents a virtual goldmine for the educated short-handed player, and the chapter that follows is what I believe to be the most informative instructional material on short-handed limit Hold'em ever put in print. The concepts in this chapter should have you well on your way to mastering these games.

Why Play Short Handed?

Short-handed poker has many benefits. For one it is much more exciting than normal ring game poker. You get to play a lot more hands, which is certainly more fun than waiting around for aces. It is also more profitable too, since you are dealt twice as many hands.

In short-handed poker you can exploit your opponents' weaknesses much more than you can in a full game, since you are more likely to be involved in hands with them and will have less interference from the rest of the table. At a full game if you have someone who calls down with way too many hands, you still have to wait a long time until you get a hand you can see the flop with to go after their money. And if a couple other players see the flop as well you can't value bet weaker holdings like you would heads-up with a calling station. In short-handed poker you might see dozens of flops with that calling station, many of them heads up, so if you get anything you can punish him.

Short-handed poker is also an excellent teacher. You see a lot more flops with marginal holdings and have to push a lot of thin edges. This is great practice for full games as it teaches you how to play in tricky spots, how to play out of position, and how to read your opponents very well. While I don't recommend short-handed poker for beginners, I do feel that more advanced players can learn a lot from it.

The Blinds

The most important change in the game is the greatly increased cost of the blinds. To see this clearly let's examine a $20/$40 game with blinds of $10 and $20. When the table has 10 opponents a round of blinds costs $30 and you see 10 hands, meaning that each hand is basically costing you $3 in ante. When the table is 5 handed you still post the same $30 in blinds, but now you have to do so every 5 hands, so you are effectively anteing $6 per hand. If you were playing 3 handed you would effectively be paying $10 per hand in ante.

As you can see sitting out now becomes much more expensive and the antes more valuable, so you have to play a lot more hands. You can no longer wait for premium holdings because you would blind yourself to death. This means that you (and your opponents) are all going to be seeing a lot more flops and doing so with marginal hands. It also means that the hands that win the pot are often going to be considerably weaker than the ones that would win at a ten-handed table.

Aggression

Since there are far fewer people at the table, it stands to reason that more pots are going to be short-handed or heads-up after the flop. Since there are fewer people seeing the flop, and those people have weaker hands than they would at a full game, there are going to be many more times when nobody hits the flop at all. And when nobody hits the player who bets first (or bets the most) is often going to be the one to pick up the pot.

Because of this, short-handed Hold'em becomes a game of aggression. Remember that an opponent who doesn't start with a pair is only going to hit a pair on the flop about a third of the time. So if you are an aggressive player and you are betting against that opponent you are going to take the pot off of him more often than not. And even when he hits something you might just hit too and beat him anyway.

So to win short-handed you are going to have to be much more aggressive than you are at a full game. You are going to have to bluff more and value bet weaker holdings. You are going to have to raise hands preflop that you might even have folded at a full table, and you are going to have to push those hands the whole way through. This is why short-handed is fun and also why it is profitable. Most people never become aggressive enough to win at a short-handed table.

Since short-handed play is such an aggressive game, your ideal opponent is a passive one. Tight passive opponents are probably the best. They play few hands and when they do they will let go of them too easily. You can steal many pots off of them. Their blinds become your profits and the blinds go around fast in short-handed games. This is why short games are so lucrative these days, since the same strategies that most books endorse using in full games, while possibly excellent advice ten-handed, tend to run a player broke at a five-handed game. Even the better full game players often become suckers at a short-handed table.

Big Cards

Because pots are being contested by fewer players and everyone is playing more aggressively, drawing hands like suited connectors lose some of their value. You are now going to have to pay more to draw at your straights and flushes and have fewer people paying you off when you hit. Because semi-bluffing becomes such a powerful play in short-handed poker they still retain some value. Also, if you are semi-bluffing with a flush draw with a hand like 8♦ 7♦ and you catch a pair it is more likely to win the pot than it is at a full table. But in general the poor implied odds still make drawing hands less valuable at a short-handed table than they are at a full table.

Conversely, pairs and big card hands increase in value. Whereas in full games a hand like 2♦ 2♣ will often be up against multiple opponents and need to hit a set to win, in short handed it will often be up against only one opponent and will be much more likely to hold up on its own. An opponent with two overcards is going to hit one by the river only about half of the time, and often you can bet him out if he does not hit the flop or turn, so you may even win with this hand more often than not.

Whereas a hand like Q♦ J♠ might have kicker troubles if it hits top pair at a ten-handed table, at a five-handed table the chances of your queen or jack kicker being best are greatly improved. At a ten-handed table if you hold that hand and the flop comes:

you are probably up against a few opponents and have to be very careful in case one of them holds a king. At a five-handed table you likely are up against one or two opponents, so the chances are much better that you have the best hand.

Aces also increase in greatly value. A hand like A♠ 2♥ is a bout a 6-4 favorite over a hand like K♦ Q♣, but it will probably win even more than 60 percent of the time if played aggressively because you will often bet your opponent out on the flop or turn. In fact you are going to have the best hand on the flop over 2/3 of the time, and even if you are outflopped you still have three outs. In a full game a crummy ace isn't likely to hold up unimproved and more people will hit flops, making it harder to bet a pot down. In a short game it can steal more and sometimes win without even pairing.

Preflop Play

In short-handed play, it isn't really as useful to define positions as it is in a full game. So for this case I will simply define early and late position. Late position is the button and the seat before it, and early position will be the other seats. If you are playing four-handed or shorter, then everything is either late position or a blind.

The most important thing to remember about shorthanded play is to never be the first limper. If you play a hand

and nobody has limped or raised yet, then raise yourself. There is no hand that you should ever call with if there is nobody in the pot. Consider a $10/$20 five-handed game. Under the gun folds and you are left to act. There is $15 in blind money currently in the pot and you limp for $10, making $25. Now suppose you put $10 more in for a raise. That $10 extra only has to steal the pot just less than 30 percent of the time to show an immediate profit.

Your raise also has many other positive effects. It makes it much harder for the button (the only player left behind you) to enter the pot, thus sometimes stealing position for you in later rounds. It seizes the initiative, which is always a good thing in poker. And if you are called it puts more money in the pot for you to win or steal later.

If you are the second player to enter the pot and the first player limped, you should raise the vast majority of the time as well. You want to get the pot down to you and the weak limper or the two of you and a blind if you can. Steal position and punish him for making a weak limp. Chances are he has very little, so make him put extra in the pot for you to steal or win later.

Don't be a passive preflop player. Whether you decided to play the hands I recommend or decide to play either tighter or looser, do so aggressively. You can't win at shorthanded Hold'em playing passively. Blind steal and isolate every chance you get. Don't let anyone in cheaply.

In any position AA-QQ and AKs or AK are capping hands. AQ suited or offsuit is a very strong hand, as are pairs

9s or better, and you should probably most always three-bet them. AJ, AT, KQ are all pretty strong hands as well, suited or not, and are okay to three-bet with against typical players.

In early-position play, I recommend playing any two cards 10 or higher. Any pair 6s or up is fine. If you are in a game full of weak-tight players, mix in the bottom pairs too. Any suited ace will do. You can play offsuit aces down to A9. Also mix in suited hands like K9s, Q9s, J9s, T9s. You can raise a few more suited hands if you like, but unless your table is pretty easy to push around I wouldn't take it far. This assumes you are raising with nobody in. With a limper ahead of you just cut out some of the weaker stuff since a blind steal is no longer an option, but still raise.

In late position with no limpers add in any two 9 or higher, suited or off. Any ace will do, suited or otherwise, as will any suited king. Any suited connectors down to 54s and one gaps down to 97s are fine as well. Any pair should go upstairs, and if you really want you could mix in even more junky suited stuff if the table is passive.

In late with a limper you should throw away most of the junky suited connectors and stick to isolating with anything I recommend playing in early with no limper. You could also mix in the offsuit Ax hands and low pairs as well if the table conditions are favorable and you have a good shot of isolating.

If there is a raise ahead of you then you are mostly going to want to three-bet or fold from any position. It is almost always well worth the extra one bet to try to get position and get the pot heads up. Just calling will make the pot inviting

to people behind you and especially the blinds, which is fine if you have a hand like 7 7, but if you are sitting on something like AJ just narrow the pot down.

That being said you are definitely going to want to tighten up against a raise, though not as much as you did in a full game. Since people raise more liberally you can and must call or reraise more liberally. Just how far you take it depends a lot on the raiser. If it is a very tight player who plays short-handed much the way he plays full games then you don't want to be three-betting with A9s or something of that nature. The last thing you want there is to find yourself heads up for three or more bets against a hand like AK, so just go ahead and fold must of your hands and three-bet only with premium holdings.

Against a maniac you would three-bet very liberally. Maybe reraise with any decent pair and any big ace or big king. Against someone like that you just want to get the pot down to you and him, and since he raises a lot of hands you don't have to worry so much about your AT being dominated. In fact a hand like that has a very good shot of being the best (and maybe even having him dominated) and can be played somewhat strong if an ace flops. Try to get the pot down to just you and the maniac if you play a hand.

Use your judgment when deciding what to reraise. Just don't find yourself isolating a player who has you dominated any more than you have to. That happens sometimes, but it is not good for you at all.

From the small blind if everyone folds to you raise just

like you would in late position. With a limper though you are going to want to be more passive since you are now out of position anytime you see a flop. So call with all of those hands if there has already been a limper. If there has been a raise you can actually just call a bit more here than you would in late position. You are, at most, going to let only one player in behind you by just calling rather than three-betting and there is no chance of your reraise earning you good position. Just how loose you should be depends on the player who raised, where he raised from (button raises garner less respect than UTG raises), and how well that player plays after the flop. Also of great importance is the size of the small blind. A small blind that is 2/3rds of the bet will make you much more inclined to call than a small blind that is only 1/2.

On the big blind you can defend pretty liberally, maybe calling with anything you would raise in late position with no limpers. Again, whether or not to defend is based on your opponents. Still you are always getting 3-1 odds or better if there is only one raise, and since it is short-handed you can usually get paid if you flop a hand. And you may have a good chance of stealing.

If you are facing multiple raises from any position tighten up just like you would facing one raise in a full game. If you have a big pair or AK, cap it. Don't call three bets cold with hands like AJ that are easily dominated. Having a good ace and hitting a flop is very expensive if someone has an even better one, so try to avoid it.

On the Flop

When the flop comes you are going to want to play very aggressive poker. If you raised preflop and only have one or two opponents who called your raise, then bet the flop. It doesn't matter what the flop is, just bet. You will take it right there enough to show a profit. This is especially true if you are in position.

I know it looks bad when you pop a hand like:

both blinds call, and the flop hits:

but consider it from your opponents' perspectives. They know you raise a lot of aces before the flop and an ace hit the flop. If they don't have an ace and you do they are a huge underdog, drawing either dead or probably to a five-outer at best. They are going to fold all of their KQ type hands. And if they take a card off with something like 89 they might even fold on the turn if you bet there, especially if something like a jack or a ten pops. And if a king or queen hits you are in position and can just check and try to show it down cheaply if you think there is a good chance they check-called the flop with an ace.

Or if you think it is good you can value bet.

Always betting is also a great form of deception. How could your opponents ever have any idea what you have if you bet every flop? They can't. They have to suspend judgment until the turn, or mistakenly narrow down your range of holdings when they really aren't able to. Either is great for you.

Against a player who bets every time here (like yourself) you have to check-raise a decent amount when out of position. You should also bet into them a lot, taking the bet away from them. You need to do both a good amount of the time and do both of them with all types of hands from bluffs on up to straight flushes.

If you get check-raised on the flop or if someone bets into you then it is time to reevaluate. With the above KQ a check-raise looks pretty bad. There aren't many good draws (just some gutshots) so the odds of a semi-bluff are low. Your hand looks like it has a good shot of being a pair of aces which is discouraging to a bluffer so the odds that they have an ace are better than average. If the person raising you has any pair at all you are a pretty big dog, and even if you turn a pair you can't play it very aggressively. And if they just have the ace they are representing, which they will a good amount of the time, you are a huge underdog, needing runner-runner to win a pot.

So in the above case you have two options. Folding would be your usual option, which you would use the vast majority of the time. Don't wait, just let go of the hand immediately. No sense even putting one more bet in there.

Your second option, which you probably only want to run if you are fairly sure they don't have an ace, is to bluff at the pot. There are two ways to go about it. One would be to three-bet the flop and follow with a bet on the river. The second would be to just call the flop and pop the turn. Both are very risky plays. In both you are investing a lot and have to be correct a fairly high percentage of the time. That is why I recommend just folding most of the time.

But if you are going to continue on then pick one of them and go with it. You might choose to wait for the turn to bluff but then call an audible and switch to just calling if you hit a king or queen, but for the most part if you decide to run that bluff follow through with it. Whether or not to choose one of those options and which one to choose is entirely dependent on the opponent and situation, but neither is very appealing most of the time.

Probably the biggest mistake I see players make at short-handed tables is continuing on with hands that are either slim or dead. Even worse is when, as in the KQ hand above, even if their hand is the best chances are a turn bet is going to force them out. Continuing on passively with a hand that could easily be drawing near dead, as our KQ is on the ace high flop, is just plain foolish. Don't draw to hands that are either drawing thin (if a king or a queen is live) or near dead. Fold them or make a play at the pot.

If you are check-raised or bet into on the flop after having the lead preflop but your hand looks to at least be fairly live then you probably don't want to let it go. Let's say you have the same

but this time the flop comes:

and you get check-raised. Now you could consider just taking one off. Your opponent could have any number of draws or just a 10. You could easily have six outs and the odds of you being dead or near it are greatly reduced. You are getting nine to one now. Any king or queen will likely give you the best hand. A jack gives you an open end, a 9 gives you a gutshot to go with your overcards, and any diamond gives you a king-high flush draw. In fact you may want to just go ahead and make it three bets if you think doing so will entice your opponent to check to you on the turn, thus enabling you to take off a free card.

Again though, adjust your play to fit your opponents. Against someone who would only check-raise two pair or better, dump your hand. It isn't worth continuing on. Against someone who check-raises any two cards, you should be much more inclined to call or reraise. You may even end up calling all the way down and winning with king high. Stranger things have happened.

When you were not the aggressor preflop, things change a bit. I mentioned earlier that you should check-raise or bet out a decent amount. The more people in the pot the more you should lean towards betting because a free card is all that much more dangerous. Check-raising really isn't a favorite play of mine but you have to do it a lot to punish people for betting automatically and to keep them from knowing you are weak whenever you check.

If you find yourself with a hand that is either way ahead or way behind bluff inducing can be a great play. For instance if you defend the blind with something like:

and the flop comes:

give check-calling some serious consideration. Another good play might be to bet the flop and then call if raised and go into check-calling mode on the turn. Or even if you are just called on the flop still bluff induce afterwards. You aren't really risking giving a hand like T9 a free card since they will probably bet anyway. Whether you check and call their bet or you bet and they call doesn't make a difference when computing your EV, just how many bets went in.

As far as when you flop trips or better goes, I recommend pounding away. I don't like to check-raise then because it seems to make people feel that you have a strong hand. Against observant opponents you have to check-raise some monsters or they will know that you don't have one every time you do check-raise, but for the most part lead out with very strong hands on the flop.

For some reason it is very fashionable to slowplay trips until the turn. You see the majority of players in every short-handed game from $1/$2 to $30/$60 do this religiously. They check-call or call the flop and then check-raise or raise the turn every single time. They are giving away so much information that way because you know any time a pair flops and they raise that they don't have trips. I recommend just pounding away with trips because of that. People expect you to play the way they do (and most players do) so when you lead out they won't give you credit for trips and will get overly aggressive with dominated hands.

Also be sure to play two pair fast on paired boards as well as the occasional bluff. People will eventually see that you often bet right out with your trips, though not until you have wrecked them with it a few times. After that you could consider slowplaying them the way that they do, but at first just go crazy with them.

Against players who do slowplay trips religiously, and that is probably 95 percent of the opponents you will run across at limits $15/$30 and below, you can use their own play as a great bluff. Check-call them on a paired flop and then check-raise the turn. People expect you to play the way that they play and that is what they all do with trips. So when you check-call the flop and check-raise the turn on a paired board they often put you on trips. You will be amazed at how often people fold. It is especially powerful because you know that the fact that they bet the flop in the first place means they don't have trips.

I should warn you to be careful. Even though the vast majority of players play trips this way not all do. The last thing you want to do is flop two pair on a paired board and shovel in a ton of money against someone who did flop it and play it fast. So be very watchful to see who does play them hard on the flop and who doesn't.

If you flop a set or a straight or better just go buck wild. In short-handed poker people will play very aggressively, so give them as much chance as you can to dump in a ton of money with few or no outs. Don't slowplay much. In fact 99 percent of players would have better results if they never slowplayed a hand again for the rest of their lives. It is a play that is correct only once in a blue moon, and even then it isn't worth much. When it is incorrect though, which is probably about 99.9 percent of the time that people do it, it is often very costly.

Most people never really try playing their monsters fast on the flop. Or maybe a couple times they flopped a full house, bet out, and took the pot down and just decided they would have been better off slowplaying. Just trust me and try leading out with all of your real big hands and capping till the cows come home. You will never go back.

Turn Play

Turn play in short-handed poker is very similar to turn play in full games. If you were the aggressor on the flop you are going to want to continue with your aggression most of the time. I mentioned earlier that people take off a lot of turns with marginal holdings in full games. They do it ten times as much short handed. Bet them out. If you bluffed or semi-bluffed on the flop then give it another shot on the turn. Just don't let up, even if the turn isn't a favorable card for you.

If you called the flop and hit a good hand on the turn now is a great time to check-raise. Doing that on the double bet round hits your opponent with a tough decision. It is also good when you bet a strong hand and get a couple callers on the flop to check-pop the turn. Your check will almost always convince someone that you were bluffing on the flop and decided to give it up. If your hand is a monster, suck what you can out of them.

Just like in a full game the turn is the street to really consider laying down a hand if you think it is beat. That isn't to say that you should fold every time someone raises you on the turn. But if you are ever going to lay down a good hand because you think it is beat, the turn is the time to consider it. If you are undecided about whether or not to continue on I suggest not doing so, especially if it seems very likely that you will have to call another big bet on the river as well.

River Play

River play doesn't really change at all from full game play, other than you can maybe even call a bit more. Like full tables you are probably going to want to continue on bluffing if you already did so on the prior two streets, especially if your opponent is likely to have a busted draw that is higher than your hand. Again your bluffs will likely fail more often than not but that is fine, they don't need to work all that often to show a profit.

Conclusion

Short-handed poker is a game of aggression, so be the aggressor. Don't play passively on any street. Use passive play to bluff induce and mix up your play a little bit, but for the most part if your hand is worth playing, it is worth betting or raising.

The increased cost of blinds forces you to play a lot of hands. The lack of players and aggressive nature of the game make big-card hands and pairs much more valuable than they are in a full game. This also makes drawing hands like suited connectors less valuable than they would be ten-handed. Adjust your preflop standards accordingly.

Don't slowplay. If you flop a monster hope someone else hits a good hand and pays you a lot. Make betting the main staple of your short-handed diet, but be sure to check-raise a decent amount so your opponents can't get any more information from your checks than absolutely necessary. Lead out and check-raise with all types of hands.

Because you are playing so many pots heads-up, knowing your opponents is of utmost importance. Watch everything that they do. Find their weaknesses and exploit them while trying to eliminate your own. Use the long-term solutions I advise in the chapter on plugging leaks to fix any problems in your game and look for people who seem unable to do the same.

Standard Deviation, Hourly Rate, and Bankroll Requirements

Depend on the rabbit's foot if you will, but remember it didn't work for the rabbit.

—R.E. Shay

I get a lot of questions from people who read my website asking about some of the statistical terms they read about in poker books. To someone who is not well grounded in mathematics, terms such as standard deviation can be rather confusing. I am going to try to explain them in layman's terms here so that you can use them in your pursuit of poker profits, but if you are mathematically inclined and wish to delve deeper into the topics check out *Gambling Theory and Other Topics* by Mason Malmuth.

The purpose of calculating win rates and standard deviations is to help us determine our bankroll requirements for a given game. I am assuming here that you have a finite amount of money which you are willing to spend on a given game and that once it is gone you are done playing. For people who don't play for a living this is not as much of a factor since if they lose it all they will probably have more money later. But even many people with day jobs like to set aside a certain amount of money for poker which can be called a bankroll.

Knowing your bankroll requirements will help you minimize the damage of the fluctuations involved in the game and avoid going broke. Because of the fluctuations, even the world's best player would go broke if he consistently played games for which he did not have sufficient funds. Even world class players have losing streaks, and money management is just as important to people playing the $2,000/$4,000 game at the Bellagio as it is to the guy beating a $3/$6 game for $5 per hour at the local Vegas Nights.

By money management I simply mean selecting games for which you are properly bankrolled, not trying foolish tricks in order to play the fluctuations to your advantage. People come up with hare-brained ideas all the time about how they can cut their losses short by leaving once they have lost a certain amount and therefore skip all of the downswings while only being at the table during their good swings. In fact they apply these same strategies to blackjack, the stock market, and just about anything else gambling related, and in the end they always go broke. Don't try to time the market in poker, just play your hours and take what comes your way. In the end every player will win exactly what they deserve to regardless of their futile attempts to alter the fluctuations.

Streaks, while definitely a reality, only occur in hindsight. They cannot be predicted and therefore cannot be used to your advantage. Many people call that money management; it isn't. Good money management means finding the game with the highest win rate that you can afford to play and playing it. Here is how to do that.

The first thing to understand is the hourly rate. Your hourly rate is simply how much money you earn in an average hour at a given game. If you played x hours of a game and earned y dollars then your hourly rate would be expressed as y/x dollars per hour. Pretty simple, right? So if I play $10/$20 for 10,000 hours and win $200,000, then my hourly rate is:

x = 10,000 hrs
y = $200,000
y/x = $20/hr

Not a bad win rate at that level. In fact in a casino someone who beats a game for one big bet per hour at that level is doing much better than most and will probably be in the top 10 percent of earners at that game. At lower limits like that you might be able to earn as much as one-and-a-half to two big bets per hour if you are an excellent player and the game is very good.

There are two types of win rates, actual and theoretical. Your actual win rate is how much you did earn. In the above example my actual hourly rate was $20 per hour. A theoretical win rate is how much you should earn. It is entirely possible that in my above example I am actually a $22 per hour winner who just happened to be unlucky over ten thousand hours. If so my actual win rate is $2 per hour less than my theoretical win rate. I could also be an $18 per hour theoretical winner who got lucky for an extra $2 per hour.

I chose ten thousand hours in the above example (which would equate to about five years of work at forty hours per week) because it is a very large sample. The larger the sample the closer your actual win rate will be to your theoretical win rate on average. There are enough fluctuations in Hold'em that the two can be very different at times, especially over short time periods.

Determining your actual win rate probably takes more time than you will ever invest. If you beat a $10/$20 game for $20 an hour there is no reason why you should play it full time for five years. You will move up in limits far sooner. Your win rate will change at the new limits because of the increase in betting and change of competition. Chances are you will never discover your actual win rate at any given level.

What you can do is discover a range in which your actual win rate lies. The longer you play, the smaller that range becomes. The mathematics behind that get a little complicated so I won't go into them here, but you can either read the book I recommended or get a good poker results program (see my website for recommendations) that will give you a range of where your win rate probably lies.

When I mention win rates from here on out I am speaking only of theoretical win rates. Just as you pay attention only to your EV when evaluating poker plays and not the short-term results, you should pay attention only to your theoretical win rate when determining bankroll requirements. This is hard to do, as estimating your theoretical win rate is very tricky. In most cases it is probably best to get a few hundred hours of play and then determine bankroll requirements from your actual rate and add in some extra money to account for errors.

The second factor we need to determine our bankroll requirements is the standard deviation. The standard deviation is a measure of the fluctuations inherent in a game. Each game you play will have its own standard deviation. The formula for the standard deviation can be found in any statistics book or with a quick Google search if you are really interested, but simply using a good poker program (all of which calculate it for you) would be much easier.

The point of the standard deviation is to allow us to determine where our results will fall over a given period of time. For all intents and purposes our results will always fall within three standard deviations of the mean in either direction. Our results will fall within one standard deviation of the mean about 2/3 of the time and within two standard deviations roughly 95 percent of the time.

So if our win rate (theoretical of course) is $100/hr and our standard deviation is $500/hr then all of our results over a one hour session will be within $1,500 of our $100 average. So we could expect results of anywhere from -$1,400 to +$1,600. Quite a swing isn't it? About two-thirds of sessions would be within a range of one standard deviation, so the majority of our sessions will end up between a $400 loss and a $600 win.

Standard deviations decrease as the sample size increases. In fact they are inversely proportional to the square of the amount of time played. So if our standard deviation (expressed in terms of $/hr) is $100/hr and we play ten hours our standard deviation now becomes:

SD = $100/(√100hrs)
SD = $100/10hrs
SD = $10/hr

So as you can see our standard deviation has shrunk considerably. Over a 100 hour period if we had a win rate of $10/hr our results for that period of time can fall anywhere from negative $20/hr to positive $40/hr, which over a hundred-hour period means we could end up anywhere between a $2,000 and a $4,000 win.

Standard deviations, unlike win rates, become accurate very quickly. After a hundred hours or so of play, your actual standard deviation should be close enough to your theoretical one to use. A very typical standard deviation for a player who wins one big bet per hour would be something like ten big bets per hour at Limit Hold'em.

Interestingly enough, one of the reasons that Hold'em is such a great game is that it has a lower standard deviation than other poker games. This is very attractive to winning players as it allows them to win more with the same bankroll. It is a large part of why Hold'em is the most popular game today.

So now we know what win rates and standard deviations are. Rather than give you the formula for computing exact bankroll requirements (which is in the recommended book if you are interested) let me give you a table of win rates and standard deviations, both expressed in terms of big bets per hour, and the corresponding bankroll, expressed in terms of big bets, needed to assure not going broke.

Win Rate	SD – 10	SD – 15	SD – 20
0.5	450	1012	1800
0.75	300	675	1200
1.0	225	506.25	900
1.25	180	405	720
1.5	150	337.5	600
2.0	112.5	253	450

So as you can see a typical 1 bb/hr winner with a 10 bb/hr standard deviation is going to need a bankroll of 225 big bets to assure not going broke. So if that player were playing at a $15/$30 table his necessary bankroll would be $6,750.

Most people recommend adding extra to this even if you aren't playing for a living just to be safe. I personally like to stick to the three hundred big bets rule. So to play $15/$30 I recommend having at least a $9,000 bankroll. For $3/$6 you would need $1,800. Of course if your hourly rate is lower or your standard deviation higher you will want to add even more.

The reason for this is that most people tend to overestimate their theoretical win rate. I once read about a survey done that showed that 85 percent of American males think they are above average drivers. By most definitions of average, that is impossible; at most, 50 percent could be above average. The same goes for poker. Just about everyone you meet will tell you that they are a winning player when in fact less than 25 percent of poker players probably win over the course of their lifetimes.

Keep in mind that for a losing player any bankroll is insufficient. If your win rate is a negative number then you will lose any amount of money given enough time. If you are content being a losing player (and the fact that you are reading this book suggests you are not) then you can at least use the above mathematics to figure out just how much your hobby can cost you over any period of time.

Moving Up In Limits

The game represents the worst aspects of capitalism that have made our country so great.

—Walter Matthau

So you have been playing for a little while and are pretty sure of your win rate. You are beating your current game for a decent amount and are considering playing higher stakes but don't know if you should. Before you make your decisions, here are a few factors to consider.

First, is your bankroll sufficient? Doubling your stakes is going to more than double the amount you need. Typically the higher the stakes, the better the players. Better competition will lower your win rate (in terms of big blinds per hour) and raise your corresponding standard deviation. The higher in limits you are, the more this will affect you. The difference between $1/$2 and $2/$4 is minimal, the difference between $10/$20 and $20/$40 is tremendous.

Don't play a game you aren't sufficiently bankrolled for. This always leads to disaster. It is okay to sometimes take a shot at a bigger game if the table looks to be a good one, but don't make a habit out of it. Players who do always end up broke no matter how good they are. Respect the fluctuations involved in the game and never forget for a moment that no matter how much skill is involved and no matter how good you are, it is gambling.

Second, are you comfortable playing for the higher stakes? When you first get to a new limit you might be nervous about the extra money you are playing for, especially if you are forced to play a game twice as big as you were. Many places don't spread anything between $5/$10 and $10/$20, so making that jump is a rather large one.

Unfortunately you don't have much choice there. Anytime you play for more money, it may make you nervous for a while. The only way to make that go away is to keep playing at that limit until it doesn't bother you anymore. You have to think in terms only of bets when at the poker table, not dollar amounts. Worrying about what you could buy with the $40 it takes to call someone down on the turn and river can only hurt you. Worry about money before and after you sit at the table, never during. During the game your only financial concern is making sure you have enough chips in front of you to play with.

It might help to periodically sit at a higher table when you feel yourself getting ready to move up in limits. I remember when I first started playing $10/$20 at the Las Vegas Nights in my home town. Coming from $5/$10 I wasn't used to having a bad day cost me $1,000 or more. It was very scary at first. Eventually I decided to take little shots at it here and there in between $5/$10 sessions, and that helped me get used to the new stakes. That was years ago, but every time I reach a new limit is still a little scary at first.

Third, are you willing to step down if things don't work out? You should be. If you jump to a new limit and lose a nice chunk of your bankroll, don't hesitate to go back to your bread and butter. It could be that the players at your new limit were much better than the ones at the old limit. Maybe you went on tilt. Or maybe you just got unlucky. In any case go back to the old game and grind up another stake, then try the bigger game again. It will always be there.

Move up in limits at your own pace. Don't feel rushed to do so. Those bigger games aren't going anywhere. If anything higher limits seem to get easier over time. Just play within your comfort zone. When you are ready to jump to a bigger game you will know it. If you feel good about it and your bankroll is adequate give it a shot; if not just be patient. It will come.

TWENTY-FIVE

Playing Poker for a Living

Baseball is like a poker game. Nobody wants to quit when he's losing; nobody wants you to quit when you're ahead.

—JACKIE ROBINSON

It is natural, after becoming a winning poker player, for many people to start to wonder why they go to work every day. Maybe after a year or two you find yourself winning more at your regular game than you make at work and you start considering turning professional. Chances are you don't really know any professional poker players and many of the ones you might know come from the old school of thought, which pretty much means they aren't saying anything about it. They often tell other people that they work in short-term investments and hide what they really do because of some mistaken notion they read in a book twenty years ago.

Times have changed greatly. Television has increased the number of regular poker players dozens of times what it was just a few years ago. People all around the world now think poker is cool. Professional poker players are looked upon as mysterious and fashionable rather than degenerate gamblers. And I never bought all that jive about hiding that you play for a living for fear of scaring players off anyway.

Everyone knows Phil Ivey is one of the best cash game players in the world, yet there is no shortage of people waiting to play him heads up $200/$400 on the Internet. So I'm going to give you my thoughts on the topic; take them for what they are worth.

First of all the decision to go pro is, for most, not to be taken lightly. For myself it was fairly easy. I was working low-paying jobs trying to save for tuition. I had no dependents and could easily find another $10/hr job to get me through the rest of my schooling. And I had a little bit of an income coming in from the Internet, so even if poker failed, I would have been able to pay the bills.

For someone who has a better job and dependents, the decision can be much tougher. My advice is to realize going in that most people, even if they are very good poker players, are going to fail at playing professionally. Be sure your kids aren't going to starve or be unable to afford college if you do fail because chances are that you will, probably within the first year.

The reason most people who try to play poker for a living fail isn't that they aren't skilled enough at the game. I would say the biggest reason is poor money management. I know of a player in my hometown who is mediocre at best but who has played cash games around here for a living for years making a decent wage. He is consistent, avoids tilting and playing limits too high for his bankroll, and puts in plenty of hours. I also know of another player in the same city who, at his best, is actually a very good player but due to tilting and poor money management can never seem to last more than a year without going broke.

So be sure to manage your money well if you do try to play poker for a living. Don't quit your day job until you have a bankroll sufficient to play in limits that will allow you to win an amount greater than what you made at your job. Remember that when you quit your job you lose all of the benefits associated with it, such as employee stock purchase plans and health benefits. Those are material benefits and are easily quantifiable. Check around and see how much health insurance will cost you once you are self employed, and be sure to add that into how much you need to earn to maintain your standard of living. Remember to account for all of the other monetary benefits your employment gave you. To really maintain the same standard of living you had while working a $50,000 per year job you may need to make $60,000 per year playing poker.

On my website I list some programs and books that will help you figure out exact bankroll requirements, and I talked a little about them already in this book. A good program can even factor in your monthly expenses when determining your needed roll. Wait until you have a sufficient amount to play a decent limit before quitting your job. A rule of thumb many people follow is 300 big blinds for any given limit Hold'em game but when playing for a living you would be well served using at least 500 plus a few months of expenses.

So if you spend $2k a month in living expenses and want to play $15/$30, then wait for a $21,000 bankroll. That may sound like a lot but trust me, you'll need it. I would guess that 75 percent of all people who fail as professional poker players do so because they were under-funded—just like entrepreneurs.

Also, you really have to be on your "A" game at all times. If you are prone to tilting, you need to fix that before you try to play for a living. When it rains it often pours in poker. If you are the sort to often let bad runs affect your play you are going to have a very hard time as a professional. People who play in casinos sometimes lose for an entire month, sometimes even two. This can be demoralizing and hard to recover from.

Other things I have seen bring good players down are alcoholism and gambling addiction. These can ruin your life regardless of your profession, but as a poker player you are more exposed to them than the average Joe. Stay away from the craps table. There is one very well-known tournament player who pretty much gambles away every cent he ever earns there. I personally never gamble on anything in a casino, and I recommend that to anyone.

Also stay away from the juice, at least while working. I never have more than a couple of drinks while playing. I really do think that a little alcohol makes anyone a better player, but a little quickly crosses over into a lot, which is disastrous. And even if it stays at just a couple of drinks, doing that every night isn't good for the old liver. Whether or not you drink socially on your own time is up to you, but while playing keep it to a minimum.

There are, of course, a ton of other vices that tend to ruin a person's quality of life but they have nothing to do with poker. Still, it is easier to fall into them when you don't have to be at work in the morning. Having a set schedule at your job really helps keep your life in line. If you want to set yourself a schedule and are disciplined enough to follow one then feel free to try it. Most people who play poker do so in part for the freedom of working whenever you want, though, and having a schedule would really ruin the experience.

With freedom comes responsibility. I can say from experience that it is pretty easy to win a very large sum and be tempted to take a long vacation. I often have weeks or sometimes even days now where I make more money than I made in a year of my last job. Still, I have to make myself keep playing. Your profit in poker is proportional to the number of hours you play, as long as you aren't playing far too many and burning yourself out. So when things are going good, don't just take the rest of the month or year off.

And that leads me to the best advice I ever received about playing poker for a living: "the best way out of a shooting slump is to keep shooting." I hear a lot of people say that when you have a bad day or week, you should take some time off. While this has a certain logic, I don't endorse it. I think you should just keep playing. If you are playing for a living, you can't afford to take a week off every time you have a couple losing days; you will spend far too much time not working. And even if you could the only way to get better at keeping your cool when things go bad is to just suffer through it.

Tilt is kind of like the common cold. Every time you get it you build up an immunity to one of its causes. The more colds you get the less likely you are to get one in the future. And in poker the more bad streaks you suffer through the less likely you are to be affected by ones later. If you feel yourself steaming it might be okay to end the day if you really can't get yourself under control, but come right back the next day playing your best. The more often you do that the stronger you will get and the less you will tilt in the future.

Also remember that playing poker for a living isn't as glamorous as it might seem on television. True, it has its moments, but the people you see on TV are mostly tournament professionals, and most professional poker players are cash game pros. Trust me when I say that the tournament life isn't all it's cracked up to be. You might see one of them win a few hundred grand and think that they are lucky. What you don't realize is that the big time tournament players can spend as much as a quarter to a half of a million dollars a year between buy-ins and travel. And if you think the bad streaks are bad in ring games wait until you have played a number of tournaments. Most tournament pros are probably more likely to lose over an entire year than I am to lose for a week playing cash games.

Most professional poker players play ring games and that is probably what you will play. Cash games are the way to go for most. You can make more money with any given bankroll there given the drastically lower fluctuations. You can set your own schedule or have none at all, whereas with tournaments you always have to be in a certain place at a certain time. As a cash game player if you want to travel if you can, if you want to stay home you can. I was just recently at a table in a WPT tournament with a player who has won two events there and travels to pretty much every stop on the tour plus many of the other major events. I asked him if he likes to travel so much and he said he hates it, which I know a lot of them do, but as a tournament player he has little choice. He can either switch to cash games or just play the tournaments in his hometown (Las Vegas) and take the other eight months or so of the year off. As a cash game player I can make a great wage staying at home if I so desire.

If you are going to go pro consider playing on the Internet. The games are extraordinarily convenient. They typically aren't as good as games of the same stakes in casinos, but since you can play multiple tables at a time and see twice as many hands per hour per table you can make a lot more with the same bankroll. Most people's per-table win rate drops slightly as they add a second or third table (and the drops become more pronounced after that), but their overall hourly rate increases.

I know there are a lot of people out there making $100-

$150 an hour playing $15/$30 online, four tables at a time. That would require a bankroll of somewhere around $10-$15k depending on the player. To make that much in a casino you would have to play at least $50/$100 and need a bankroll of somewhere north of $30k. And the $50/$100 games in casinos are definitely going to be, on average, much tougher games than the $15/$30 games online.

So you can see that at low to middle limits, playing on the Internet is just more profitable. In a casino you are at a fast table if you see forty hands per hour. Online playing four tables you might see three-hundred hands per hour. As far as win rates go, casinos just can't compete.

Internet playing is often boring though and you may want to play in casinos as well. That leaves you with the option of traveling often or moving somewhere that has casinos or cardrooms if you don't already live near them. Traveling gets to be very expensive and moving may not be an option depending on your family situation. Consider that before you quit your job as well.

Playing poker for a living is a wonderful life for those who can live it. Someone motivated enough can make literally hundreds of thousands per year sitting in front of their computer with a little skill. Poker right now is a money tree ripe for the shaking. The level of play seems to be on the rise so the money is slowly becoming harder to win, but there is still plenty to be made for a skilled player and there always will be. When the economy takes a downturn the gaming industry generally experiences a surge, so the job is recession proof. And best of all you can't get laid off as a poker player.

The freedom is the best part. I set an alarm clock only a few times a year, and then generally just so I will wake up in time to catch a plane. I don't have any boss to answer to, and I work whenever I want. When I am sick I don't have to call anyone. I spend a lot of time in Las Vegas, my favorite place on Earth. I get to meet a lot of interesting people and have actually made a few good friends that way. And I have much more time to spend with my girlfriend and all of my friends than I ever had before.

Poker really is a hard way to make an easy living. I hate to quote that old phrase but it really is true. If you think you are one of the few who can pull it off, then go for it. Most poker pros advise people not to try it, but they aren't looking at it from a poker perspective. If you minimize the risk of failure and the loss you suffer from failing, you greatly increase your pot odds so to speak. Just be sure that if you fail you don't put yourself in a very bad position. Always leave yourself an out.

Odds Chart

Chances of making a hand on the turn, river, or with both left to come.

Turn River Combined

Outs (percent) (X:1) (percent) (X:1) (percent) (X:1)

1531.92.1332.62.0754.10.85
1429.82.3630.42.2851.20.96
1327.72.6228.32.5448.11.08
1225.52.9226.12.8345.01.22
1123.43.2723.93.1841.71.40
1021.33.7021.73.6038.41.61
919.14.2219.64.1135.01.86
817.04.8817.44.7531.52.18
714.95.7115.25.5727.82.59
612.86.8313.06.6724.13.14
510.68.4010.98.2020.43.91
4 8.510.758.710.50 16.55.07
3 6.414.676.514.33 12.57.01
2 4.322.504.322.00 08.410.88
1 2.146.002.245.00 04.322.50

% = percentage chance of making your hand on the turn,river or combined
X:1 = odds to 1 against making your hand

Common Draws

Outs:	Hand:
15	Open ended straight flush, flush draw with two overcards
14	Straight draw with two overcards
12	Inside straight draw, flush draw with one overcard
9	Four flush
8	Open ended straight, double gutshot straight
5	Pair (drawing to two pair or three of a kind)
4	Gutshot or two pair (drawing to full house)

Glossary

all-in: To put in the last of one's remaining chips in a table stakes game. Doing so means that a player can not win or lose any more than he had in his stack to or from each individual opponent. So if a player goes all-in for $5 he can only win up to $5 from each opponent; anything more wagered by those opponents goes into a side pot that the all-in player cannot win.

aggressive: Indicates a lot of betting and raising. A player or a game can be said to be aggressive.

bad beat: When a hand that is a favorite loses to a hand that is an underdog.

bankroll: How much money you have to play poker with.

bet: *v.* To be the first player to increase the bet above $0. *n.* The current wager. *Ex.* "The bet is $5."

big blind: The larger of the two forced wagers on the first round of betting. In limit Hold'em this is almost always equal to the size of the wager on the first two rounds of betting. It is always live, meaning it counts toward the poster's wagering requirements for the round in which it is posted.

blank: An insignificant card that is unlikely to change the outcome of the hand.

blind: A live, forced wager on the first round of betting. Generally played in lieu of antes to stimulate action. There are almost always two of them in limit Hold'em,one small blind and one big blind.

bluff: To bet or raise with a hand that has little or no chance of being the best in order to make all opponents fold.

brick: See Blank.

button: A small white button, usually labeled "Dealer," that rotates around the table to indicate position. The player with the button in Hold'em is last to act in every round of betting.

buy-in: The amount of money a player starts with.

call: To place into the pot an amount equal to the current bet or less if all-in.

check: To remain in a pot without putting in any money. This is only an option if nobody has yet bet.

steam: *See* Tilt

stone cold nuts: A hand that is the best possible hand on a round of betting and cannot be beaten or tied later. This differs from the nuts because the nuts can lose on a later round of betting or only tie another player with the same hand.

straight flush: Five cards of consecutive ranks all of the same suit. Very rare in Texas Hold'em.

suck out: To draw out on a hand.

suited: To be of the same suit. A♥ K♥ is generally referred to as ace-king suited.

suited connectors: Two cards of consecutive rank and of the same suit. An example would be 5♣ 4♣.

table stakes: A game in which a player can go all-in and only money sitting in front of a player on the table can be used to play. In most table stakes games there is a minimum buy-in, and taking money off of the table is not allowed. In games that are not table stakes players may bet any amount they wish, whether it is in front of them or not, and another player must either call it, raise, or fold. No player can go all-in. Almost all games played nowadays are table stakes.

tell: A physical mannerism which gives one's opponents a clue as to the player's hand.

three of a kind: Three cards of the same rank. This can be made either using two cards from a player's hand and one from the board (see Set), one card from a player's hand and two from the board (see Trips), or with three cards from the board.

tight: Indicative of not many hands being played. Either a game or a player can be said to be tight.

tilt: A loss of discipline generally caused by bad beats. A player on tilt usually plays a lot of hands and takes them way too far.

trips: Three cards of the same rank using two cards from the board and one from a player's hand. An example would be if a player held A♦ K♣ and the flop was A♣ A♥ 3♦. The player would be said to be holding trip aces. Trips are generally inferior to a set.

turn: The third round of betting in Texas Hold'em in which a fourth community card is placed on the board. In limit Hold'em the turn is usually marked by a doubling of the wager.

underdog: A hand that is not the favorite to win the pot.

under the gun: The first player to act in a round of betting. Generally used to refer to the player following the big blind preflop in Texas Hold'em.

unsuited: Containing different suits, generally used to refer to hole cards. A♦ K♣ would be referred to as ace-king unsuited. Also it could be called ace-king offsuit or just ace-king off for short.

value bet: To bet a hand that has a good chance of being the best hand hoping for a worse hand to call.

Index